A GUIDE TO
RACE-GOING

A GUIDE TO RACE-GOING

Martin Diggle

J.A. ALLEN

First published in 2018 by
JA Allen

JA Allen is an imprint of
The Crowood Press Ltd
Ramsbury, Marlborough
Wiltshire SN8 2HR

www.crowood.com

British Library Cataloguing-in-Publication Data
A catalogue record for this book is available from the British Library.

ISBN 978 1 908809 73 5

Photographs by Colin Wilby and John Barlow, except where otherwise
credited. All photographs are copyright of the owner.

Typeset by Jean Cussons Typsetting, Diss, Norfolk

Printed and bound in India by Parksons Graphics

Contents

Acknowledgements

I would like to express my thanks to the following people who assisted me in the writing and illustrating of this book.

I am grateful to Joe Rendall and Lyn Williams of the British Horseracing Authority (BHA) for their help in responding to my queries on various points of detail regarding current rules and regulations of racing, and to Willie McFarland, Genny Haynes and Debbie Burt who, on behalf of the Arabian Racing Organisation, provided me with some updated details of that branch of racing.

My long-time friends Carolyn Henderson and Colin Wilby kindly offered to read through my draft chapters. From their different perspectives both provided perceptive comments that were a great help in fine-tuning the text, and Colin provided many of the photos that appear in this book. London Racing Club member, John Barlow, also supplied a number of photos and I am most grateful for his generosity and support.

Thanks are also due to the following contributors of photos: the public relations staff at Cheltenham racecourse, for a photo of a race over their cross-country course; Les Hurley, who provided photos of all-weather racing at Wolverhampton and fixed-brush action at Worcester; Nigel Kirby, who provided a photo of a pony race on behalf of the Pony Racing Authority; and Ginni Beard, who provided two photos of point-to-point action and one of pony racing at a point-to-point meeting. The photo of Arabian racing is by GeptaYs/Shutterstock.

AUTHOR'S NOTE

Since I am very fond of horses and understand that they are sentient creatures with their own personalities, I dislike them being referred to as 'it', and prefer to use personal pronouns. Since the vast majority of horses engaged in racing are male, this book uses the forms 'he' and 'his' as an expedient when referring to 'the horse' generally. However, where, from the context, the reference is clearly to a filly or mare, the appropriate feminine pronoun is used.

From a human perspective, until fairly recent times racing was very much a male-dominated sport, with areas of active prejudice against females. Fortunately there have been major changes through the last few decades and nowadays there is widespread female involvement in all areas of training, riding and management. This being so, my general use of male pronouns to refer to trainers, jockeys, etc. may invite comment but, again, it is done purely to avoid clumsy sentence construction and I hope that it will be excused on these grounds.

Preface

The late spring sunshine has brought a bumper crowd to what is, in any case, a popular race meeting and, in truth, the weather and the competitive racing are major factors in your own attendance. It's early in the flat season, many of the horses are making their seasonal debut, and there are some tight handicaps, so you're here to enjoy the spectacle, rather than seek your fortune – it's a day simply to enjoy the experience.

They're off, and a last-minute queue for a pasty has left you out of position for optimum viewing. You find a small gap by the rails and crane forward. Nothing to see as yet but, gradually, you become aware of a rhythmical drumming, which starts to get louder. Shortly, you are aware of other sounds: heightened breathing; the occasional slap of a whip, an odd hissing sound, which some jockeys use to encourage their mounts to further efforts and – yes, one jockey asking for room in less-than-polite terms. Then, almost in an instant, your field of view is flooded with a kaleidoscope of colour – reds, blues, greens, yellows, purples and many more in various combinations on the jockeys' silks, and greys, chestnuts, bays and browns of the horses' coats, now streaked with sweat and gobbets of saliva. It's like a DVD switched to fast-forward – it's hard to take in how fast these horses seem to go when you're up close to them. The question crosses your mind: 'If they're all going that quick, how does one ever manage to overtake another?' You make a mental note not to panic if, at a later date, you back a horse who needs to be settled off the pace.

*   *   *   *

A different scenario: a dull, damp and misty day in late November. The cloud cover helped disperse the overnight frost rapidly, but it hasn't raised the air temperature overmuch. You can't remember quite how many layers you put on, but you're damned glad of all of them – especially the waterproof jacket. Those clonking great hiking boots that usually lurk unnoticed in the front porch were a good spot, too.

The upcoming race is a 2 mile 6 furlong novice chase – not the greatest ever run, and not the safest to bet on, but the almost black ex-hurdler caught your eye in the paddock; he looked fit and keen for his first run over the bigger obstacles. Your knowledge of his hurdles form tells you that he could be a bit of a sketchy jumper back then, so there's a question mark over how he'll cope with fences, but he's got a good trainer and jockey, and his hurdles form also suggests that he'll cope with the ground and get the trip. He's worth a small bet, for interest.

Of course, once the tapes go up, you find yourself considerably more nervous than his jockey, who risks much more than your fiver riding novice chasers most days of the week. As the race unfolds, you realize that you have everything crossed and, when your fancy meets the first open ditch on an in-between stride and climbs over it rather unconvincingly, you get an object lesson in what arrhythmia means. However, bar a length lost, all is well; the field continues on its way, with your horse still in touch.

Well into the final circuit and, as they turn into the straight with two to jump, your horse has moved into second place, and begins to press the leader. His jockey has settled into a deeper position in the saddle, and is beginning to push away, but so is the rider on the long-time leader. In fact – yes, yours seems to be going slightly better. Hell's teeth – please let his jumping hold up now. Surely, it's just the exaggerated holding of your own breath that gets him over the fence, and he's now a length ahead, but his jockey has started to ride in earnest and the former leader is hanging on gamely under extreme pressure. Please, please don't 'miss' the last. He's a bit far off it on the final stride – not ideal for a tiring ex-hurdler having his first run in a chase, but he bravely takes off out of the jockey's hands, gets sufficient height and lands running. The run-in is just 200 yards, but uphill on dead ground it seems to take an age. Another runner, staying on from further back, is closing, but has too much to do. Yours crosses the line two lengths ahead, and you feel a sudden need to sit down. Bad for the heart – but good for the soul. Where's that hip flask?

Introduction

Today, more and more people are going to the races. There may be many reasons that trigger a first visit – a day out with friends, to accompany a partner, the attraction of a post-race concert by a favourite band, simple curiosity, or a long-time intention finally coming to fruition – to name just a few. For most people, initial visits will be full of surprises – the sheer speed at which horses gallop, the proximity at which they race, the noise when a race is in full flow, the flashing colours and the excitement of the crowd may all exceed expectations, as may the clear joy on the face of the lad or lass leading up the winner – a fellow being with whom they have established a deep relationship over many early, frosty mornings before first light.

So, there's a lot of excitement to engage with – and if a lucky first punt has paid for the entry fee, so much the better. But, for those new to racing, many questions will arise. Horse racing is a sport with a complex history that has given rise to many idiosyncratic traditions, and it has developed a language all of its own, spoken automatically by everyone engaged in it.* Furthermore, it is a sport whose key performers are not human, but highly tuned animals, with their individual characteristics, quirks, strengths and vulnerabilities. It is a sport in which split-second binary decisions can spell either triumph or disaster. To fully appreciate racing, to gain an insight into what really is going on, it is necessary to penetrate beneath the surface and begin to engage with the sport as a whole. The aim of this book is to assist enthusiastic newcomers to do this.

---

* For this reason, the final chapter, Racing Terminology, is essentially an expanded glossary. In most books that have them, a glossary is simply a list of brief definitions of terms used within the main text. In this book, I have turned the glossary into a final chapter and used it not just to give basic definitions, but to provide further explanations about what may lie behind these definitions. Terms that are explained in this final chapter are set in bold the first time they are used in the main text. There are also a number of terms in the chapter that don't appear in the main text, but are included to offer explanations of terms that you may hear or read elsewhere.

CHAPTER 1

Background – a Potted Guide to How Racing and Thoroughbreds Developed

Horse racing, in various forms, probably originated soon after people began to ride and drive horses, but the modern, highly organized sport of racing Thoroughbred horses is relatively recent in historical terms. To a very significant extent, the breed and the sport developed hand in hand, and what follows is a basic explanation of how this came about.

In bygone times, wealthy and enthusiastic owners of horses they considered fast ran them in races – sometimes two-horse 'matches' against like-minded rivals, often for large sums of money, on a simple 'bet my horse can beat yours' basis. There were also more-or-less impromptu races at the popular country fairs, often organized by horse dealers, and all these early races seemed to have attracted crowds of spectators. While those who liked to race their horses did make rudimentary attempts to produce faster stock, sometimes by the use of stallions from places such as Spain, Italy and Arabia (a catch-all name for a region now consisting of many separate states), there was little real science behind these efforts and there was, for centuries, no such thing as a definable 'racehorse breed'.

THE DEVELOPMENT OF BREEDING RECORDS AND PRACTICES

During the sixteenth and seventeenth centuries, things began to change. In the reign of Henry VIII two royal studs were established, overseen by an Italian horsemaster named Prospero d'Osma. Although these studs had the aim of producing better-quality horses, and the stock produced were grouped into three 'types', there were no early records of the actual pedigree of the individuals, and no clear evidence that they were bred specifically for racing – though it is highly probable that some of them had an influence on the sport.

In the period following Henry's reign, the royal studs were supported by the Stuart kings, James I and his son Charles, and this era saw further introductions of foreign stock, although there is still little evidence of an advance in a cohesive breeding strategy at this time.

James I was the first monarch to establish Newmarket as a sporting centre and – although it was initially used mainly for hunting and falconry – racing began to flourish there. However, following the reign of his son, Charles I, and in the aftermath of the Civil War, racing throughout England stalled for a while because the government of the day banned it. This was ironic because the Lord Protector, Oliver Cromwell, who was basically a country squire, enjoyed racing – the ban was not a puritanical move on his part (although it was perhaps considered as such by some members of his Protectorate), but was motivated by the thought that, in uncertain times, he wished to discourage large gatherings – which may be further evidence of racing's long-standing attraction as a spectator sport.

The restoration of the monarchy in 1660 saw an upturn in the fortunes of both Newmarket and racing generally. The new king, Charles II was, in modern parlance, 'mad for it', to the extent that he moved his court to Newmarket for months on end and endeavoured to govern the country from there – with mixed results. He, himself, rode in a number of 'matches' with some success and, not surprisingly, his enthusiasm for the sport ignited a similar enthusiasm amongst many members of the gentry.

One of Charles II's early equestrian measures was to re-establish the concept of a royal stud (which had been dissolved during the Protectorate years) under a royalist named James D'Arcy. D'Arcy had already gained a reputation as a breeder of good horses at his Yorkshire estate and, finding the old royal stud in ruins, he suggested an arrangement that was seemingly mutually beneficial to himself and the king. This entailed D'Arcy supplying the king annually with twelve 'extraordinary good' foals from his own estate, for a pre-arranged sum, which meant that he could, in effect, 'work from home', whilst saving the king the costs of resurrecting and running a costly premises of his own.

For various reasons, which seem uncertain, but suggest a muddying of the waters on both sides, this arrangement unravelled in time and, following D'Arcy's death, Charles moved the royal stud to a new base at Hampton Court. Following this, the late D'Arcy's son (also James), spent many years petitioning the monarchy (on Charles' death, James II, then William III and Mary) for some kind of monetary compensation he believed his family was owed, to no effect. However, documents produced to support his petition suggest that more thought was being given to breeding practices, and confirm a growing emphasis on importing horses variously described as Barbs, Turks, Persians and Arabians – in short, horses from the eastern and southern Mediterranean regions.

Although D'Arcy's documents shed some light on how horse breeding was developing, it was still the case that records, generally, remained both scarce and uninformative for some decades to come. For one thing, there was no centralized repository; more importantly, such records as did exist were largely imprecise, at best. Hard-and-fast records of the pedigree of any individuals were rare, and the very identity of many horses was uncertain. This was because horses often weren't given names, as we would understand them, but were referred to in such terms as 'Lord X's Barb' – which, upon sale or loss as a gambling debt might, overnight, become 'Mr Y's bay'! Even if a horse was given a name, this could be changed at random, with no notification. It is no surprise, then, that many aspects of the genesis of the Thoroughbred are uncertain, and remain subject to speculation and debate among even the keenest students of the subject.

The man whose work was most influential in laying the foundations of better breeding (and other) records was John Cheny. Initially, Cheny had been approached by a group of wealthy owners and asked to travel the country with the chief intention of recording race results, and some of these owners had asked that the pedigrees of the horses also be recorded. Cheny did try to comply with the latter request, but travelling constraints and the impromptu nature of many race meetings meant that he had his hands full trying to ensure that he got the bare results right and, given the virtually random nature of horse-naming in that era, and the idiosyncratic nature of pedigree records (where they existed), he did well to record the odd snippet relating to the parentage of a featured runner. His first publication, *Historical List of Horse-Matches Run* (1727) was far from being a comprehensive record of breeding, but it was the first step down an important road.

For some years, Cheny struggled to improve his work on an annual basis. Initially, he faced the same problems as previously but, during this era, an increased interest in the business of breeding led to an increased demand for information about it, and to the promotion of the services of various stallions. By 1743, Cheny was able to produce an annual far more detailed than his early efforts – although, even then, he felt it necessary to include comments and cautionary notes in relation to many of the details he recorded, saying, in effect, that the accuracy of some might be uncertain.

By the time Cheny died in 1750, the importance of his work was widely appreciated, and his title was taken over by Reginald Heber. In 1756 *Heber's Historical List* contained a significant page, headed 'A Pattern for a Stud Book'. While he may have got the idea for this from prominent breeders of his acquaintance, he certainly understood the value of complete, accurate records, and the publication of this page seems to have been influential in encouraging breeders to be more conscientious in their record-keeping.

Heber's final volume of the *Historical List* was published in 1768 and, following his death, there was a struggle as to who should be the key provider of racing and breeding information. A man named Benjamin Walker tried to keep the *Historical List* going, but he was unable to compete with another journal, *The Sporting Calendar*, produced by William Tuting and Thomas Fawconer, both of whom were officers of the Jockey Club. (Interestingly, although the Jockey Club was to be the guiding force in the organization and development of racing, its precise origins are rather obscure. It evolved from a group of sporting aristocrats who met at the Star and Garter in London's Pall Mall, and seems to have been founded officially in 1750. Soon after this, the club leased a coffee house in Newmarket as a base for their racing interests.)

Although *The Sporting Calendar* beat off the *Historical List* in commercial terms, there were complaints from subscribers about omissions. With Tuting and Fawconer taking on new roles within the Jockey Club, both their old roles were taken over by James Weatherby, formerly a solicitor. Weatherby, who seems to have had a sharp head for business, manoeuvred *The Sporting Calendar* from their grasp and began to publish his own version, the *Racing Calendar*. However, with what was initially a monopoly on journals of its type, he did little at first to improve the content, and its future might have been uncertain had not a rival publication appeared on the scene in 1786. This publication was William Pick's *Sportsman and Breeder's Vade Mecum*, which included details then absent from *The Sporting Calendar*. Pick had already produced a work called *Pedigrees and Performances of the Most Celebrated Racehorses*, which incorporated stud book plans similar to those of Heber, and his new publication was a serious rival to Weatherby's.

This challenge seems to have caused Weatherby to sharpen his focus. Perhaps overstretched by trying to handle both his Jockey Club work and his own business, he called in his nephew (also James) to help with the publishing side of things. This was the genesis of what was to become a family business, whose close links to breeding and racing continue to the present day.

Although the younger James certainly played a major role in the development of Weatherby's company's publications, early success was facilitated by William Towers, a subscriber to the *Racing Calendar* but also an admirer of Pick's work and a man who had begun to compile lists of pedigrees for his own purposes. It was Towers who first had the idea of producing a *General Stud-Book* (the hyphen was later dropped), which was initially advertised by the younger Weatherby in the *Racing Calendar* of 1790. Perhaps wary of the mixed reception given to previous publications about breeding, Weatherby referred to the first work as *An Introduction to a General Stud-Book*. However, Towers' authoritative preface emphasized his commitment to eradicating the problems of incomplete and inaccurate information that still tended to bedevil breeding records, and his layout of information within the book proved more reader-friendly than most journals that preceded it. For a time, Towers' work faced a serious challenge from the continued output of William Pick, who remained a significant contributor to the development of pedigree records. Before long, however, readers interested in breeding began to favour Towers' format and, in due course, this was recognized by Pick himself. Although authoritative works on Thoroughbred breeding continued (and continue) to be produced by various authors, by the end of the eighteenth century the *General Stud-Book* had become established as the key source of information on breeding records, and continues to fulfil this role today.

THE DEVELOPMENT OF THE THOROUGHBRED

As stated earlier, the development of the Thoroughbred was intrinsically linked to the establishment of pedigree lines and stud records and, just as the latter were becoming established over time, so was a specific type of racehorse developing. It is sometimes stated that the Thoroughbred owes its existence to three stallions, the Byerley Turk, the Darley Arabian and the Godolphin Arabian and, in fact, all members of the breed trace back in their male line to one or other of them – however, they could not have had the same degree of (admittedly remarkable) influence without the assistance of essentially well-bred mares. These three stallions arrived in England in, respectively, 1689, 1704 and (around) 1730. The Byerley Turk was probably an old breed called the Akhal-Teke, highly regarded in Asia; the Darley Arabian came from Syria, and was known to be from a strain of horses bred specifically for racing; and the Godolphin Arabian had an uncertain history and an even more uncertain start to his role as a stallion. He was used by his owner, Edward Coke, as a 'teaser' for his stallion Hobgoblin. (A 'teaser' is a warm-up act, sometimes used to get a mare in the mood to be covered by the intended stallion.) With Hobgoblin disinclined to do his duty with a mare named Roxana, the Godolphin Arabian stepped into the breach and sired a highly successful racehorse, thus launching his own career.

As will be seen from the brief descriptions given, these three horses represented the kinds of foreign bloodlines that various breeders had been introducing to cross with native stock for many decades. With increasing interest in racing, the desire for fast horses was also accelerating and, even if the planning of bloodlines and the early record-keeping might be described, in many cases, by terms such as 'chaotic', 'idiosyncratic' and 'experimental', there was an overall improvement in the type of horses produced. Although most early breeders seem to have placed primary importance on the male line of pedigrees, matings inevitably produced fillies as well as colts, so it can be argued that the tendency towards better stock applied to both sexes. With general progress in the type of horses available for breeding, the influx of especially influential stallions, and more thought being put into breeding plans, a particular type of horse was beginning to emerge. One thinker on these matters was John Lawrence and his book *The History and Delineation of the Horse* (1809) was one of the first to use the term 'Thoroughbred' to apply to the English racehorse.

If we can say that (although it continued to develop) the breed had been established by that date, it is worth having a look at the type of races that had been run previously, and how things began to change.

DEVELOPMENTS IN RACING ADMINISTRATION

The work of the first James Weatherby, both in his roles as Jockey Club official and in promoting the *General Stud-Book*, served to found a dynastic connection to racing that continues to this day. In addition to registering all Thoroughbreds in Great Britain and Ireland, Weatherbys (they do not use an apostrophe) administers racing under contract from the British Horseracing Authority (BHA), and provides a wide-ranging number of services connected with the sport.

The BHA is nowadays the chief administrative body of racing in the UK. In many respects it is something of a descendant of the Jockey Club, although the latter still exists. When the Jockey Club came into existence, its initial main aim was to establish set rules of racing on Newmarket Heath. These proved very successful and were, in due course, adopted elsewhere. Over time, the club became the official governing body of racing in Britain with, as stated, administrative support in certain areas from Weatherbys.

In the 1960s, the Jockey Club branched out and began to acquire racecourses (initially Cheltenham, in 1964 – currently fifteen) with a view to securing their future. This process continued and, in 1993, there was structural change whereby a new organization, the British Horseracing Board (BHB) was established to be the main governing body of British racing while the Jockey Club retained its roles in connection with rules and regulations.

Race Measurements

When racing was developing, all measurements in the UK were imperial and this inevitably meant that all race distances were given in miles and parts thereof. In addition to quarters, halves and three-quarters, other parts of a mile were given in furlongs, one furlong being one-eighth of a mile. This tradition has continued – virtually all references to race distances are in this form, although some racecards now give metric equivalents in the main race heading. The use of imperial units also applies to weights carried by the horses, which are given in stones and pounds.

The Jockey Club had, since its inception, been a self-elected body, with many members having 'vested interests' in racing in terms, for example, of horse ownership. Becoming aware that such bodies can be open to criticism, and wishing to increase regulatory independence, they were party to the inception in 2006 of a new organization, the Horserace Regulatory Authority (HRA), which took on the 'policing' role while the Jockey Club focused more on matters such as the administration of the National Stud (formerly in government ownership), encouraging investment and generally promoting racing through various initiatives. The ability of the Jockey Club to participate in these roles was enhanced when, in 2008, the BHB and HRA merged to form the BHA.

DEVELOPMENTS IN RACING

Nowadays, on the flat, any race of 2 miles or longer is considered a 'staying' race and there are only a handful of races of 2½ miles or more during the whole season. During the early days of organized racing, things were very different: many races were run in a series of 'heats', and a single heat of 2 miles would have been considered short. At Newmarket, the distance of the Beacon Course was around 4 miles 1½ furlongs. With such extreme demands on stamina, it is not surprising that horses of this former era were rather different from modern Thoroughbreds, since stamina requires a different type and blend of muscle fibres than does sheer speed. However, the speed with which the breed was evolving is well indicated by the influence of three horses born within a couple of decades of each other: Matchem (b. 1748); Herod (b. 1758); and Eclipse (b. 1764). All three began their racing careers at the age of five (another indication of how flat racing has changed) and all were successful over the aforementioned Beacon Course. However, significantly, all three went on, as stallions, to sire horses capable of winning the newly established Classic races for three-year-olds, the St Leger (inaugurated 1776, approx. 1 mile 6 furlongs), the Oaks and the Derby (inaugurated 1779 and 1780 respectively, both 1½ miles).

From the latter part of the eighteenth century onward, the old, long-distance races began to be phased out, and there was increasing emphasis on speed and shorter distances. By way of example, two further Classics for three-year-olds, the 2,000 and 1,000 Guineas (1809 and 1814), both over 1 mile, were established at Newmarket, making something of a contrast with the former Beacon Course races. From the early nineteenth century onward, there has been a general tendency to place increasing emphasis on speed in breeding racehorses, and flat races of 1¼–1½ miles are nowadays generally considered 'middle-distance'.

Until the first part of the nineteenth century, the vast majority of horse races took place on the flat: there is little documentary evidence of much racing over obstacles before that era. Two factors that may have stimulated interest in racing over obstacles were the increased interest in fox-hunting as a sport, and the various Enclosures Acts, which stimulated the construction of various barriers by which to turn what had previously been common land into distinct fields. Perhaps the most influential of these was the 1773 Act, but many others followed and, with an increasing availability of obstacles, sporting riders felt inclined to jump them (or attempt to do so).

One of the first recorded races over obstacles took place in Cork, Ireland, in 1752. The course of approximately 4 miles ran across country from Buttevant Church to St Leger

Church, with the steeple of the finishing church being an obvious landmark and guide. It is thought that this was the origin of the term 'steeplechase', later widely adopted and still the 'official' term for races over the larger obstacles. It is also believed that, in 1774, a race was run at Newmarket that included a series of substantial obstacles, but the first recorded steeplechase in England took place in Bedfordshire in 1830, over a 4-mile course. (Interestingly, the recorded time for this race was sixteen minutes twenty-five seconds; modern Grand Nationals, over a little further, are usually won in under ten minutes.)

Not long after the Bedford race, in 1837 an hotelier from Liverpool had the idea of staging a spectacular steeplechase that, in 1839, at the revised venue of Aintree, became the Grand National. In the early days, the Grand National course included an area of plough, a stone wall and, ironically, a hurdle as a final obstacle and, as steeple-chasing grew in popularity, other courses initially included features natural to the area on which the races took place. There was, in fact, little in the way of regulation of this branch of racing until the 1860s, which saw the establishment of the National Hunt (NH) Committee and the development of a programme of races over 'regulation' fences at various courses, some of which remain at the forefront of the sport today. In due course, jump races subdivided into the larger steeplechase fences and the smaller hurdles. One of the most important hurdle races in the earlier days was the Imperial Cup, first run at Sandown in 1907.

Jump racing is the province of older horses than those who commonly compete on the flat, and races take place over longer distances. Whereas a 2-mile flat race is a 'stay-ers' event, this is the minimum distance for hurdles and steeplechases, and many of the biggest steeplechases are run over 3 miles or further.

As National Hunt racing developed, so did point-to-pointing, or amateur steeple-chasing. This, in fact, was also rooted in the idea of gentlemen racing each other across country, as with the early steeplechases, but it quickly became closely associated with individual hunts, there being a requirement that owners of point-to-pointers be subscribers to a hunt, and that the horses be 'regularly and fairly hunted' in order to be eligible. By the 1880s this branch of racing had become popular to the extent that it threatened to eclipse the professional sport, and the National Hunt Committee stepped in, imposing various rules and regulations, some of which seemed idiosyncratic, to say the least. One was that no point-to-point course should be 'defined', which accentuated the connection with the original cross-country steeplechases. It wasn't until the early years of the twentieth century that courses started being marked out with flags. By the 1920s, birch fences, very similar in form to those used in professional jump racing, had been introduced to most courses. It was also during this decade that something very surprising happened – male point-to-point riders found themselves compet-ing against female riders, the National Hunt Committee rules not having specifically banned the latter. As a result, there was a series of grudging amendments that first introduced restrictions then gradually yielded concessions until most point-to-points were open to both male and female riders – although there are still some 'men's opens' and 'ladies' opens' for reasons other than simple discrimination. (Female jockeys were not allowed to ride in professional races until a series of advances in the 1970s.)

In recent times, point-to-pointing has been managed and administrated by the Point-to-Point Authority (PPA), which functions under delegated authority from the BHA. The PPA has seven directors: three are independent; and there are one each from the

Jockey Club; the Point-to-Point Owners and Riders Association (PPORA); the Point-to-Point Secretaries Association (PPSA; and the Masters of Foxhounds Association (MFHA).

DEVELOPMENTS IN RACE-RIDING TECHNIQUE

Historically, while breeding programmes, Thoroughbreds and racing administration were all advancing, one thing that did not advance for centuries was the riding style of jockeys. Going back to Medieval times, much of the riding had been in military style, with armoured knights sitting upright, bracing themselves in deep saddles, with their legs thrust forward to withstand the shock of opponents' lances. Even once full armour and lances became *passé*, a similar seat was useful for exchanging sword blows from horseback. Very severe bits were used, partly in an attempt to prevent terrified horses bolting, and partly to exercise the absolute control necessary to minimize the chance of sudden decapitation. (Away from the battlefield, some riders practised high-school dressage as an art, using a similar, although more refined, posture to exercise precise control of their horse's movement.) As a result of this background it was normal for people (at least for military men, the nobility and servants employed by them) to ride in a style typified by an upright body and long stirrup leathers (and thus long legs), employing bits that, in simple terms, were more fitted to stopping horses than encouraging them to gallop freely 'into the bridle'. Looking back, it almost beggars belief that people riding in races followed this style from – let's say the Tudor period, which is where we embarked on this history of racing – almost to the end of the nineteenth century.

There are various problems with riding in this style when the aim is to have horses galloping to the maximum of their ability. One is wind resistance from the jockey, but there are more significant issues, including the rider's weight bearing on the horse's back rather than being positioned above it, and the fact that, at gallop, for much of the time the horse's centre of gravity will be in front of that of a bolt-upright rider. So far as jump races were concerned, this rider's position makes the desirable task of going 'with' the horse over a fence virtually impossible, and the fact that riders participated in such races in the position described says, I suppose, a good deal about their courage, but nothing about any understanding of equine biomechanics. One supposes that the horses must have exhibited a good deal of fortitude, since it is likely that they often had to deal with a rider hanging on by their back teeth during the act of jumping.

The person who instigated change was an American jockey named Tod Sloan, whose revolutionary style was noticed, and initially mocked as a 'monkey seat', when he came to ride in England. Sloan is generally believed to have adapted his own style after watching African-American stable lads in his home country riding more or less kneeling on their horses' withers and realizing that their horses moved faster and more freely when ridden in this way. (This is probably true in Sloan's case, but it seems that a somewhat 'forward' style had been used many years before his time by riders of Quarter Horses – very fast non-Thoroughbreds raced over short sprinting distances, particularly a quarter of a mile, hence the name.) Since, on a visit to Newmarket in 1898, Sloan rode five consecutive winners, the mocking soon stopped, and it wasn't long before British jockeys began to approximate to his style. Pictures from the Edwardian era show jockeys in postures considerably different from those of a couple of decades earlier, although, compared to modern jockeys, they are still riding with very long legs. However, over time, the standard 'jockey position' developed further, until we see the very short leathers in evidence today, with very streamlined jockeys perched above their mounts. Perhaps ironically, there is a view that, nowadays, some jockeys ride so 'short' that the benefits are countered to, some extent, by their having limited ability to use their legs to help drive their mounts forward or to hold them straight if they begin to '**hang**' in the closing stages of a race. Whatever the view on this, such jockeys remain of almost infinitely more benefit to their mounts than their counterparts of a previous era.

More History

If you are interested in discovering more about how horses and racing developed, there are many avenues to explore.

The National Heritage Centre for Horseracing & Sporting Art at Newmarket (www.palace-housenewmarket.co.uk) includes a racing museum, a gallery of sporting art and a chance to meet retired racehorses in the Retraining of Racehorses establishment.

The 'Heritage' section of the Jockey Club's website (thejockeyclub.co.uk) includes a potted history of the club's development, and many racecourses' own websites also contain a brief history of the course.

In addition to producing articles for various magazines, a number of eminent racing journalists have written highly informative books giving historical perspectives on breeding racehorses and the evolution of the sport. There is no space here to give a comprehensive list, but a few works I have found informative include those of Peter Willett, Christopher Poole, Tony Morris and John Hislop. In addition to being an owner and breeder (and writing on those topics), John Hislop was a top amateur rider. Although, in some respects, a little 'of his time', his textbooks on race-riding (*Steeplechasing* and *Flat Race Riding*) contain much that remains valid and will be of particular interest to anyone wanting to learn more about various aspects of jockeyship.

CHAPTER 2

Types of Racing

As we saw in Chapter 1, in the early days, virtually all racing took place on the flat, with racing over obstacles becoming more popular, and more regulated, through the years of the nineteenth century. In this chapter, we'll look at the various types of racing available today in more detail.

FLAT RACING

The flat racing season traditionally runs from early spring until mid-autumn, and this continues to be the case in respect of the major races and how such things as jockeys' and trainers' championships are decided. However, with the advent of suitable artificial surfaces, meetings can and do also take place during the winter months.

Flat racing has traditionally taken place on turf courses, and most flat courses remain in this form. One drawback to this is that weather conditions can materially alter the state of the ground (possibly affecting the size of fields) and, in extreme circumstances, render it unraceable, leading to widespread inconvenience to all concerned, and loss

A flat race on turf with a good covering of grass. The divots indicate that the horses are racing on a fairly soft surface. (If you intend to watch racing close up in these conditions, choose your footwear wisely.)

of revenue. For these reasons, there are now several courses with artificial 'all-weather' surfaces. These, with proper maintenance, allow racing to take place on a more-or-less standard surface in pretty much any British climatic conditions. The materials used for these all-weather courses are, nowadays, also used by trainers (of both flat and jumping horses) to provide training surfaces that offer an alternative to their grass gallops during adverse weather conditions, thereby avoiding hold-ups in the training programme, or the risk of working horses on unsatisfactory surfaces. Despite the role of all-weather surfaces in training jumping horses, all racing over obstacles takes place on turf – hurdle racing on artificial surfaces was trialled briefly in the 1990s, but the surface used at that time proved unsatisfactory for jumping at racing speed. That said, you may occasionally see jumping horses crossing short stretches of all-weather surface on courses that combine (turf) jump racing with all-weather flat racing, and the jumps-only course at Fontwell now has an all-weather stretch on the bottom bend, but no obstacles are taken on that section.

In England, both Wolverhampton and Chelmsford racecourses are dedicated all-weather flat-racing tracks, with floodlighting to permit evening meetings. Some other courses, such as Kempton, Newcastle and Southwell have replaced their former turf flat course with all-weather surfaces, although they retain turf courses for jump racing. Lingfield, one of the pioneers of all-weather racing, has many of its meetings on that surface, but still has some flat racing on its turf track, and also has a jumps track.

In the early days of all-weather racing, most of the meetings consisted of fairly low-grade events, and it had a general reputation of being 'second class'. However, for some years now, it has been attracting better horses to compete for bigger prizes and some courses have transferred old-established, high-prestige races from their now-defunct turf tracks to their all-weather replacements.

An all-weather training gallop.

All-weather action under floodlights at Wolverhampton racecourse. (Photo: Les Hurley, for Wolverhampton racecourse)

Although, as stated, most trainers now work their horses on both all-weather and turf surfaces, and although some horses race on both these surfaces, the **official (BHA) handicappers** may sometimes allot different ratings for a horse's turf and all-weather performances, because some horses act better on one surface than the other.

Flat races in the UK take place over distances from 5 furlongs up to the 2 miles 5 furlongs 143 yards of Ascot's Queen Alexandra Stakes.* In simple terms, races of 5 and 6 furlongs are designated as sprints, races of around 1–1½ miles are 'middle-distance' and races of 2 miles upward are 'staying' races. The 'in between' distances are rather subject to interpretation, although 1 mile is considered significant, with a number of top races taking place of that distance. As with human athletes, most horses perform to their optimum at a specific distance, or within a relatively small range of distances. Seven furlongs is often a specialist distance – horses who perform to their optimum at this distance are often just a little outpaced at 6 furlongs, and don't quite stay 1 mile. On the 'staying' side, there are some horses who seem to perform equally well at distances from 1¾ up to 2½ miles, whereas others who do well at the shorter **trip** only just stay 2 miles.

---

* The precise distance is given here to illustrate a relative innovation in how race distances are presented. The race was formerly referred to as being 2 miles 6 furlongs, but race distances were remeasured following some revisions to the layout of the course. Elsewhere, similar, more accurate measurements have taken place on other courses and racecards nowadays often show precise distances of races – for instance a '5-furlong' race may be given as, say 5 furlongs and 17 yards, or a '2-mile' steeplechase may be given as, say 1 mile 7 furlongs 197 yards.

Thoroughbreds' Birthdays

Thoroughbred horses, rather like the British monarch, have two 'birthdays'. Officially, they all become a year older on the first day of the calendar year. In practice, they are nearly all born in the spring, but, for official purposes, both a foal born in March and one born in May will turn 'two' on 1 January in the year at which they are actually yet to attain that age. Because an earlier foal may have developmental advantages over an older one, breeders try, so far as possible, to synchronize a mare's receptivity to breeding with calendar dates that suggest an early foaling but, with nature always having a final say in such matters, the best-laid plans sometimes backfire. However, while logic dictates that late foals are likely to be at a disadvantage compared to their earlier peers (and while this often results in the former being given more time before their careers begin in earnest), such 'disadvantage' is not always evident in practice.

On the flat, there are races for horses from two years old upward. (There is no official upper age limit at which horses can race in either flat or jump racing but, as with human athletes, age is usually a major factor in loss of performance and flat racing, with its accent on speed, is generally a younger horse's game – although perhaps not the extent that is often assumed. Horses racing on the flat aged nine or ten are not common, but neither are they especially rare.) Because Thoroughbreds generally develop and mature rapidly, and are expertly reared and trained, most of those bred to race on the flat can do so at the age of two, provided their racing programme is mapped out judicially and paused in the light of any setback. Early in the season, two-year-old races are run at 5 furlongs, with longer races being added as the season progresses. This doesn't mean that all two-year-olds are obliged to race over the longer distances; simply that such races become available. A mile is usually considered a long race for two-year-olds, although there are a few later in the season over distances of up to 1¼ miles for potential staying types.

Two-year-olds don't usually race against older horses, but there are a few important sprint races that allow this, with any such entries getting a **weight allowance** from their older rivals.

For three-year-olds, there is a broadly similar progression of race distances through-out the season. In addition to the sprint distances, most early-season three-year-old races are at around 1–1¼ miles, with more at around 1½ miles during the lead-up to the early summer Classics, the Derby and the Oaks, at that distance. Later in the season, there are races specifically for three-year-olds at distances up to 2 miles, and sometimes staying types may take on older horses in late-season handicaps at distances in excess of this.

From the age of four upwards, flat horses will race at whatever distance(s) seem to suit them best.

All flat races (with a very few rare exceptions in particular circumstances) are started from starting stalls, the intention being to ensure a fair, even start for all runners. However, not all horses are equally adept at leaving the stalls promptly and sometimes a jockey who needs to get some **cover** in the early stages of a race will deliberately give away a little ground at the start in order to manoeuvre in behind other runners to prevent his mount being too free early on.

NATIONAL HUNT RACES

The term 'National Hunt' (NH) describes all races that take place under NH rules and, for the most part, encompasses races over hurdles and steeplechase fences – known informally as 'over the sticks'. The jump racing season has traditionally run from autumn through to spring, and this continues to be the case for all the major events. A main reason for this is that, generally speaking, ground conditions are more likely to be suitable for racing over obstacles during this part of the year – landing over obstacles at speed places significant concussive forces on horses' limbs if the ground is firm and the general expectation is that, in the UK, it is more likely to be rain-softened during autumn, winter and spring than in summer (although, of course, with the British climate …).

That said, there has been a good deal of work done to many courses (both flat and jumping) in respect of both watering and drainage, and there is now more early-season jump racing, with some bigger prizes on offer, than was formerly the case, and a tendency to put on some evening meetings both in spring and early autumn, to take advantage of the available light. The need for **connections** of jumping horses to be prudent with regard to ground conditions notwithstanding, it is a fact that some horses, by virtue of their **conformation** and **action**, perform better on a sound surface than in a winter bog, and these individuals often show their best form early or late in the jumping season.

National Hunt Flat Races

As stated above, the vast majority of NH races are run over obstacles of one sort or the other, but there are also some flat races run under NH rules, as features on what are otherwise jumping programmes, commonly as the final race of the day. Typically run over distances of about 2 miles, these races are primarily intended to give potential jumping horses some racing experience before they start to race over obstacles, although there is no official requirement for them to do so. Because they are intended to have an educational role there is a limit to the number of times a horse can run in them (usually four, unless a fifth and sixth race are high-level 'pattern' races). Although education is a main criterion of these races, they are subject to the normal rules, and there is betting on them. Nowadays, such races are included on the programmes of some highly prestigious meetings, such as those at the Cheltenham Festival and the Aintree Grand National Meeting.

Since they are run under NH rules, these races, in common with all hurdle races and steeplechases, are started by flag from behind a barrier. Consequently, there is no draw for starting position.

Hurdle Races

Hurdles are built of wooden panels filled with brushwood, and are similar to the obstacles formerly used as temporary barriers to keep livestock in fields. Approximately 3½ft in height, they are hammered into the ground at a slight angle, leaning away from the direction in which they are approached, which makes their vertical height a few inches lower. (In all forms of equestrian jumping, an obstacle that slopes a little like this is more inviting for the horse and easier for him to 'measure' than one that is upright.) At some racecourses, there is a dedicated hurdles track but, because their placement can be temporary, on other courses they are positioned on the flat course, at times when there is no flat racing.

The relatively flimsy nature of hurdles, and the manner of their placement in the ground, means that, if they are hit hard, they may sometimes be knocked flat, but this does not mean that a horse making a bad mistake in a hurdle race cannot fall, if his balance or momentum is severely compromised.

Hurdle races take place over distances from 2 miles up to 3 miles plus – in a few cases as far as 3 miles 3 furlongs. The official requirement is that there must be a minimum of eight hurdles in a 2-mile race so, on average, there will be four hurdles to a mile.

There are some hurdle races confined to three-year-olds, which take place late in the calendar year, when the horses are getting towards their fourth year; these are usually over the minimum distance for the course concerned – nominally 2 miles, but at some courses the layout is such that the minimum distance may be a little further than this. (As an alternative, there are some handicap hurdles run from July onwards designated for 'three-year-olds upward', which gives a trainer an option to get a young hurdler into handicap company once he is eligible to be handicapped and if that route seems appropriate for that individual's career.) There are also races restricted to four-year-olds (and sometimes, four- and five-year-olds). Beyond these restrictions, most races are open to all ages. Most of the horses who go hurdling can be very broadly divided into two types: those moving on to it from a flat-racing background (who will tend to make up the majority who start hurdling at three), and later-developing types who might, in due course, go on to run in steeplechases. Some the graduates from the flat may well continue to have a career that mixes flat racing with hurdling, and this brings us to an interesting phenomenon.

A flight of hurdles.

   Most horses who move on from flat racing to hurdling will have been running over somewhat shorter distances on the flat than they face over hurdles – this is because hurdle races are run rather more slowly than flat races, and the act of jumping (if done efficiently) gives horses a moment's respite from relentless galloping. Therefore, a 'dual-purpose' horse who runs in 2-mile hurdle races will typically race over a distance (give or take a little) of around 1½ miles on the flat, and a horse who stays 2 miles plus on the flat may well stay 3 miles over hurdles. Therefore, there are basic differences between the two **codes**. However, leaving aside the stamina differential, which has been explained in principle, the fundamental difference for a horse between running 1½ miles on the flat and running 2 miles over hurdles is the presence of eight (occasionally nine) obstacles – approximately one in every quarter mile. This being the case, it would be reasonable to expect that a horse would show a similar level of form whether on the flat, or over hurdles – and some horses do so. It would also be easy to understand that, if a horse didn't take to jumping (whether mentally or physically), his form over hurdles would be inferior to that on the flat – and this again is sometimes true. What is less easy to explain is that, sometimes, a horse will prove to be *very much better* over hurdles than on the flat. Two prime examples of this, from the past, were Persian War and Night Nurse. Although both were quite moderate performers on the flat, both were top class over hurdles, Persian War winning the Champion Hurdle three times and Night Nurse winning it twice. Something very interesting also happened to a rival of Night Nurse's, a horse called Sea Pigeon. In the early part of his three-year-old career on the flat, he was highly regarded and ran pretty well in the Derby. Later in the season, however, his form tailed off and he was labelled difficult and highly strung. After being **gelded**, he was sent hurdling and began to show better form, which continued on an upward trend. A decision was made to try him again on the flat, and he won three major handicaps (the Chester Cup twice and the Ebor) carrying big weights, before going on to become another dual Champion Hurdler. Sea Pigeon was a pretty complicated character, and there were probably many factors other than the simple switch to hurdling linked to his subsequent progress, but the stories behind all three of those mentioned underscore the fact that horses can be complex creatures.

   After a while, many (though not all) hurdlers are introduced to steeplechasing. If and when this happens are decisions left to the judgement of their connections but, generally speaking, most trainers who want to make the change prefer to do so after just a couple of seasons. This sort of time frame gives horses a reasonable amount of racing experience to take on to the bigger obstacles and (assuming they started hurdling at around four) some time in which to mature mentally and physically. On the other hand, it means that they are less likely to have their hurdling technique so deeply ingrained that they find it difficult to make the adjustment to jumping bigger fences. This is a significant consideration because, although it is always helpful for horses to jump hurdles quickly and cleanly, they are more likely to get away with the odd bad jump over these obstacles than over steeplechase fences. Furthermore, a horse who has an ingrained instinct to take off a long way from his hurdles and jump them fast and flat when asked for maximum effort in the final stages of a race, may revert to this method when under pressure in a steeplechase, and risk a heavy fall. Therefore, moving on to steeplechasing before too long a career over hurdles can have its advantages.

   Occasionally, whether for psychological or physical reasons, a horse will struggle with the transition from hurdles to steeplechasing and, when this becomes apparent, wise connections will revert to the smaller obstacles sooner rather than later, to avoid risk of injury and/or a loss of enthusiasm on the horse's part. A prime example from the fairly recent part was a horse called Big Buck's [sic], who had shown great promise over hurdles but looked to be the type to go right to the top as a steeplechaser. In fact, he didn't really take to the bigger obstacles and was soon switched back over the smaller ones, going on to enjoy a lengthy career as an outstanding staying hurdler.

Steeplechases

Steeplechases take place over substantial obstacles built of vertical sections of brush tightly packed into robust frames. The standard height on the take-off side is 4ft 6in, although some fences on some courses are rather higher than this (an example would be the Grand National course at Aintree, where some fences are a little over 5ft high). On the take-off side, standard ('plain') fences have a 'belly' or slope away from that direction that, like the slope applied to hurdles, makes jumping a little easier and more inviting for the horses.

In addition to plain fences, steeplechase courses incorporate 'open ditches' in a ratio of about one in six obstacles. The term is perhaps a little confusing, because an open ditch consists of a shallow ditch several feet wide in front of a standard-sized fence, without the slope associated with a plain fence. This slope is unnecessary because the ditch (which has a very low rail in front of it as a visual guide) requires the horses to take off at least the width of the ditch in front of the actual fence. Jumping an open ditch places additional demands on accuracy and effort compared to a plain fence,

This view of steeplechasers taking a standard fence shows its construction clearly.

An open ditch.

A water jump.

and these obstacles look pretty formidable to an observer on the ground. However, it is enthralling to see the ease and power with which good horses, well ridden, will fly these fences.

Some steeplechase courses also include water jumps. These used to be a standard feature of steeplechases, but fewer courses include them nowadays. Where they remain, this will be on the basis of one such jump in a complete circuit so, in shorter races on longer circuits (e.g. a 2-mile chase at Newbury), **the field** will jump the water just once. Water jumps consist of a more or less upright low brush fence (a minimum of 3ft high) on the take-off side (to get the horses in the air), followed immediately by a 9ft spread of water. As with open ditches, this can seem quite a big spread to an onlooker, but horses who take off on a good stride will clear the water jump easily, with little apparent effort. In case a horse makes a mistake and lands in the water, the water itself (and, more importantly, the ditch containing it) is just a few inches deep, to minimize the chance of injury.

The general requirement regarding numbers of fences overall is that there should be a minimum of twelve in a 2-mile race, and six in each subsequent mile.

Steeplechases take place over distances from 2 miles up to just over 4¼ miles (the Grand National, the longest steeplechase in the UK, is currently run over a distance of 4 miles 514 yards). Some races allow horses as young as four to take part, but not many do so because (although there are exceptions) for the most part they have not yet reached a sufficient level of maturity.

Although horses can and do get away with making the occasional quite serious mistakes in steeplechases, in order to run to his maximum potential it is necessary for a steeplechaser to jump cleanly and fluently as often as possible. Although some horses, by temperament and/or physique, are extravagant jumpers and can look spectacular when all goes well, they can be the type who jump ten fences in a row in breathtaking

The horse carrying red and yellow colours and wearing blinkers has dived at the fence, brushing through it, and the jockey has sat back and 'slipped the reins' (let them go long).

A fixed brush race at Worcester. (Photo: Les Hurley, for Worcester racecourse)

fashion, then blunder their chances away when the wheels finally come off. (In a way, this is a bit like downhill ski-racers who know they have to take all the chances if they are going to win, and either pull it off in spectacular fashion or end up tangled in the safety netting.) Ideally, jumping trainers (and jockeys!) prefer a horse to learn to adjust his stride on the approach to a fence so that, if necessary, he can either take off a little further from it than normal and make an extra effort or, if he is likely to be too far from the fence, put in a shorter stride and pop over neatly. The latter course of action will lose him a little ground compared to a rival who jumps extravagantly, but he'll get to the other side safely, with only minor loss of momentum. (Interestingly, although the Grand National has been won by horses who were quite extravagant jumpers, on the whole the course is better suited to 'clever' jumpers – the prime example being the three-time winner Red Rum, who was never spectacular but hardly ever 'touched a twig'.)

Fixed Brush Races

Fixed brush races are relatively new to the UK, although the obstacles are similar to those that have been used in French jump racing for many years. The jumps are a kind of halfway house between hurdles and steeplechase fences and a key intention is that they provide a stepping stone for horses between the two forms of jumping. They are of similar design to traditional steeplechase fences, but smaller, generally portable, and filled with artificial 'brush' made of plastic, rather than the real thing. Similar obstacles have become popular among some trainers as a means of educating their horses at home. At the time of writing, the two courses that currently hold races over these obstacles are Worcester and Southwell.

Cross-Country Races

A relatively new addition to NH racing in the UK is cross-country racing, which takes place over long, winding courses that include a variety of obstacles such as hedges, wooden rails and banks, more commonly associated with eventing than racing. Such races have been popular in some European countries (especially France) for many years, and are also a feature of Ireland's Punchestown course. A sponsored cross-country race was inaugurated at Cheltenham in 2005 and such races now take place at several Cheltenham meetings, over a distance of 3 miles and 7 furlongs.

The nature of these races is such that they suit an adaptable, well-balanced horse, able to cope with changes of direction, and to jump the various obstacles in the appropriate manner. It is not surprising that these races often throw up 'specialists', who run well in them time after time. Interestingly, however, they often seem to revitalize horses who have 'gone off the boil' in conventional steeplechases. There may be several factors involved here – the length and twisting nature of the course means that races are inevitably run more slowly than conventional steeplechases, which may appeal to older horses who are losing a little speed and getting fed up with racing flat out just to stay in contention, and the variety of the course and obstacles may simply generate renewed interest (horses, like people, often perk up for doing something different).

CATEGORIES OF RACES

In addition to their long-established names (the Derby, the Cheltenham Gold Cup, etc.) and possibly a sponsor's name, races are given weird and wonderful designations and categorizations. This last category, although it may convey useful information regarding eligibility, prize money and status to the connections of horses, is likely to be baffling to most people. The following are lists of race types for flat and jump racing as identified by the BHA, with just very brief additional explanations for information.

Action from Cheltenham's cross-country course. (Photo: Cheltenham racecourse)

Categories of Flat Races

Pattern races – divided into Groups 1 (highest category) to 3.
Listed races – basically the category below Group 3.
Conditions races – usually a fairly high standard of race that is not a handicap, a maiden, a selling or claiming race.
Conditions stakes – as above, and not confined to apprentice or amateur riders, or with a total prize fund below a certain level.
Classified stakes – weight-for-age race that is not designated a maiden or novice race, open to horses who (although it's not a handicap) have achieved a handicap rating as specified in the conditions of the race.
Maiden races – these are for horses who have yet to win a race under the code of the race in question (thus a horse will be a maiden on the flat if he hasn't won a flat race, even though he may have won over hurdles, or vice versa). Maiden races can be sub-divided into open maidens, maiden handicaps, maiden auctions (and median auction maidens) and rating related maidens.
Novice races – oddly, on the flat, the term is specific to two-year-olds. A novice flat race is restricted to horses who have not won more than two races, who have not won a class 1 race, or more than one class 2 race; a novice auction race has the same qualifying criteria and the horse must have been sold at public auction; a median novice auction is as above, except that the final criterion is that the horse must be the progeny of a stallion whose yearlings have sold at a specified median price.
Handicaps – races in which horses carry different weights as allotted by the official handicapper. They are graded by number; the lower the number, the higher the quality. Some top handicaps are designated as heritage handicaps; nursery handicap signifies a race for two-year-olds.

Selling and Claiming Races

These races, which are not specifically mentioned under the categories, are rather unusual in that they can be seen as a means of offering the runners for sale. After a selling race, the winner will be auctioned there and then, and all the other runners may be claimed (bought, effectively) for a value set by the trainer at the time of entry. After a claiming race, any horse (including the winner) can be claimed for the set value. Since these races are pretty low-grade affairs and the claiming values are usually quite low, it can be assumed that the connections of most of the runners are pleased enough to pass them on. Regarding the winners of sellers, there has sometimes been quite vigorous bidding at the auction, on the assumption that a particular horse might be capable of further improvement. In cases where the connections of a selling race winner have wished to retain the horse, they have had to top the bidding for their own horse, a process known as 'buying in'.

Categories of NH Races

Pattern races – similar to the flat designation; top-class races divided into Grades 1, 2, 3.
Listed races – basically the category below Grade 3.

Classified stakes – a weight-for-age hurdle or steeplechase that is not a designated maiden or novice race, open to horses who (although it's a handicap) have achieved a handicap rating as specified in the conditions of the race.

Novice – under NH rules, this has a more complex meaning than on the flat. In respect of a steeplechase, it applies to a horse who, prior to the start of a season, has not won a steeplechase before 30 April of the year in which the season begins (e.g. for the season 2018/19, has not won a steeplechase prior to 30 April 2018). In respect of a hurdle race, the same criteria apply. Note that these criteria are specific to steeplechasing and hurdles rather than applying to jump races generally, so, for example, a horse who had won a hurdle race but not a steeplechase prior to 30 April would still be a novice for steeplechasing purposes (and vice versa).

A novice hunters' steeplechase – a weight-for-age race confined to amateur riders and horses who have a hunter's steeplechase certificate but who, prior to 2 June of the *previous* year, have not won a steeplechase.

A hunters' steeplechase – a steeplechase confined to amateur riders and horses who have a hunter's steeplechase certificate.

Maiden – a race confined to horses yet to win a NH race.

Beginner's – a steeplechase for horses yet to win such a race other than a point-to-point.

Juvenile hurdle – a hurdle race for three-year-olds.

Handicap – as on the flat, hurdle or steeplechase races in which horses carry different weights as allotted by the official handicapper. They are graded by number; the lower the number, the higher the quality.

As you can see, even with the briefest explanations these individual designations can be quite daunting. However, these various definitions can be grouped into broader types, whereby it is easier to understand why horses in the same race may be carrying different weights – weight variation (where applicable) being the means by which horses of presumed different ability can be competitive with each other (*see also* Handicaps below).

Level Weights and 'Level Terms' Races

These, by definition, are races in which all runners carry the same weight. There are actually relatively few of these, and they will be races in which all entries are of the same sex and there is no age allowance involved. An example would be the Oaks, a Classic race for three-year-old fillies only. Level weights races tend to polarize into being either high-class affairs aimed at the top performers in various categories, or races for relative newcomers, at a stage of their careers when there is insufficient evidence to rate them rationally on past performance – examples being early-season flat races for two-year-olds, or juvenile hurdles.

In addition to these races that are factually 'level weights' affairs, there are other races in which the underlying *intention* is that all runners compete on 'level terms', but the actual weights will be adjusted to take account of age and sex differences between the runners.

The idea that younger horses will be less mature than older ones has been long established, and the corollary that follows from this is that if young horses are to be competitive against their elders there needs to be a weight allowance (weight-for-age) to compensate for this. This does not apply to *all* races involving horses of different ages, but to non-handicaps on the flat in which two- and three-year-olds may compete against horses older than them, and to some young horses in NH races (for example, four-year-olds – who are 'young' in steeplechasing terms, may receive an allowance in some races). The precise arithmetic behind age allowances is complex (and subject to debate and periodic adjustment), but it can include factors such as race distance and time of the year (the supposition being that younger horses need less of a weight allowance as they mature).

Whereas weight allowances trace back to the mid-nineteenth century, sex allowances, whereby mares and fillies receive weight from colts and geldings in non-handicaps, are a relatively new concept. Currently, they receive 7lb in any relevant NH race and, on the flat, 3lb in a pattern race and 5lb in other grades. (This doesn't apply in handicaps – in these races, mares and fillies will carry the weight dictated by their actual rating – and thus past performances – the assumption being that this will already account for any perceived 'sex difference'.)

To give an example of how age and sex allowances can impact on a race in which the intention is that horses compete on 'level terms', a mid-season, middle distance flat race for horses of both sexes, aged three upward, could have four categories of weight carried:

Highest weight carried by male horses aged four upward.
Next weight carried by female horses aged four upward (get sex allowance).
Next weight carried by three-year-old male horses (get age allowance).
Next weight carried by three-year-old female horses (get age and sex allowance).

Conditions Races

These are usually quite high-class races, commonly a little lower in grade than the top-class level weights affairs. In these, while the age and sex allowances described above will be factors when relevant, there are likely to be other weight differences according to the specific conditions of the race. These weight differences will not be based on handicapping, but on whether horses have incurred penalties for previous successes in specified types of races, or perhaps are entitled to a weight allowance because they are yet to win a race of the current grade, or a race of a certain value. With all these variables in the melting pot, there may be a range of actual weights carried in such a race, and it can be useful to read the race conditions on the official racecard (these are often in either the front or back pages) to establish why the runners are carrying different weights. Ironically, given all the potential permutations, it would be possible for all runners in a conditions race to be at level weights if there were no differences in respect of age or sex allowances, and they all had a similar racing history.

One category of race that is essentially a conditions race, in that the weights carried depend upon a certain condition, is the auction race. These races are mainly for two-year-olds on the flat and the weights allotted are based on the prices paid for them when purchased at public auction – the more they cost, the higher the weight carried. Since there is not necessarily a relationship between how much a horse costs and his actual performance, these races tend to be a conundrum for most punters, but can be attractive to connections who think, on the basis of a horse's homework, that they've got themselves a bargain.

Handicaps

Handicaps are races in which horses are allotted different weights (within the scale of a particular race) on the basis of their official rating, which is determined by past performances in relation to other horses. The task of determining and adjusting horses' ratings is undertaken by BHA handicappers.

Handicaps are the most prevalent type of race, on the basis that they are most relevant to the greatest number of horses. As with human sport and athletics, it is obvious that only a few performers can be really top-class so, if the rest are to have any realistic chance of success, they need to compete within a system that offers an opportunity to do so. Handicaps are thus popular with the connections of the majority of horses, with those responsible for organizing races (on the basis that well-framed handicaps are likely to attract good-sized fields), with race-goers (who generally want to see the same thing) and with bookmakers (because while big-field competitive handicaps are attractive to punters, they are difficult races to solve).

Even though the very best horses rarely run in handicaps, there is still a big difference in ability between the best handicappers and really moderate horses. This means that it is impractical to frame any race to include horses at both ends of the spectrum, because the weight differences necessary would be unachievable. (There is only so much weight a racehorse can be asked to carry, and there is a practical minimum to what a jockey can weigh.) This means that handicaps are designated as different classes, with class 7 being the very lowest and the class increasing as the number decreases.

The weight range in jump racing handicaps is generally top weight 11st 12lb and bottom weight 10st. On the flat, there are more variables, but the top weight is commonly 9st 12lb or 9st 7lb, and the bottom weight 8st. (In some races, known as limited handicaps, the weight range will be less by virtue of the bottom weight being higher than normal – in a NH race for example, it might be 10st 7lb). The top weight in some races may be a little higher than the 'norms' just suggested if the terms of the race dictate this. Also, a runner may carry less than the official bottom weight if the rider is an apprentice/conditional jockey claiming his allowance. For instance, if a horse is allotted 10st in a handicap steeplechase, and his rider can claim 5lb, the horse can actually carry 9st 9lb. On the other hand, there are some circumstances in which a horse who is a little 'out of the handicap' is still able to take part. In such circumstances, a horse who has a rating that equates to say 9st 12lb in a jumping race may take part but, unless he is ridden by a claiming jockey, he will have to carry the minimum of 10st, so he will be what is known as '2lb wrong'. This will sometimes be indicated on a racecard as 10st 0lb (9st 12lb).

OTHER TYPES OF RACING

In addition to mainstream flat and jump racing, there are other types of racing that are worth a look, both on their own merits and because, to a significant degree, they relate to, or feed into, these main codes.

Point-to-points

Currently managed and administrated by the Point-to-Point Authority (PPA), with close ties to the BHA, point-to-point races are amateur steeplechases with a close association with the world of hunting. Traditionally, they are mainly hosted by individual hunts, and usually take place on land owned by someone who has a connection with the hunt (although there are a few courses shared by several hunts). They may also be organized by the Armed Forces or other bodies approved by the BHA. In days gone by, many courses were pretty rough and ready, sometimes including areas of ploughed land and obstacles not encountered in modern-day steeplechasing (post and rail fences, walls, hairy hedges, etc.). Nowadays, however, the obstacles are more or less identical to steeplechase fences, although typically slightly smaller (current regulations say that they must not be less than 4ft 3in high).

Riders in point-to-points must be a minimum age of sixteen, and must possess a rider's qualification certificate signed by the Master of an affiliated hunt, and a medical record book issued by the BHA. Riders range from the 'keen to have a go' people who may have only a handful of rides in a season, to experienced regulars who may also ride under NH rules in hunter chases, or even against professionals. (Some of the latter do, in fact, go on to achieve success as professional jockeys.)

To be eligible to run in point-to-points, horses must be owned by someone at least sixteen years old, who takes responsibility for the horse's welfare regardless of who trains him (trainers of point-to-pointers do not have to be licensed in the same way as professional trainers), and must (with the exception of horses running only in hunt members' races) be registered with the Racing Calendar Office. The horse also needs

There are many proficient practitioners in the amateur sport of point-to-pointing. (Photo: Ginni Beard)

to have a certificate on which the Master of a hunt verifies the owner's membership of that hunt. (It used to be the case that, to be eligible to run in point-to-points, horses had to have a certificate from a hunt to declare that they had been 'regularly and fairly hunted', but this requirement has now been modified.)

Horses can run in some point-to-points from the age of four upward, with some races framed for younger, less experienced horses being run over 2½ miles. (The majority of point-to-points are run over 3 miles, with a few being as long as 4 miles.) Many of the participants are horses moving on to the amateur sport following a career in professional racing, and some experienced former steeplechasers enjoy quite lengthy careers as 'schoolmasters' in point-to-points, racing on perhaps into their mid-teens. However, there are rules relating to how soon a retired horse who has been successful in NH racing can 'convert' to the amateur sport. The other side of the age divide is that younger horses who show a lot of promise as point-to-pointers may move on to hunter chases or even join the ranks of the horses in professional jump racing.

Point-to-point races are divided into a number of traditionally named categories, which stipulate the horses (and, in some cases, the riders) eligible for each. Common categories are member's, maiden, intermediate, confined, restricted and open, the last-named usually attracting the highest-class horses from the widest area. Point-to-points are usually 'conditions' races, in that the actual weight carried by an individual horse may be determined by penalties for previous successes and/or allowances including, where appropriate, age and sex allowances. Specific conditions for each race are detailed on the racecard, point-to-point racecards being broadly similar to those provided at NH courses.

The main point-to-point season runs from the New Year through spring. While racing typically takes place in attractive rural locations, many of the courses are quite close to

A pony race at a Godstone point-to-point in Surrey illustrates the relationship between these two branches of racing, and shows the pleasant rural setting often associated with point-to-pointing. (Photo: Ginni Beard)

towns and this form of racing is well worth a visit. A fixture list is available from various websites, including the PPA one and Weatherbys, and local meetings are usually advertised in advance at the roadside near the venue. At a point-to-point you will find betting options, loos, and food and drink outlets. However, because point-to-point courses are often on working farmland and have few, if any, permanent structures, you should bear in mind that shelter may be at a premium and take this into account if you are thinking of attending in inclement weather. The overall atmosphere is informal and there is ample opportunity (subject to exercising common sense) to walk around the course to view starts, fences, etc. Dogs are usually welcome, but must be kept on a lead. Regarding entry, it used to be the case that entry on foot was free, but there was a charge per car (for parking). However, in recent times some point-to-points have switched to charging a per person entry fee.

Some point-to-points play host to pony races, which usually take place at the beginning of the afternoon, so it can be worth turning up early to watch these.

Pony Racing

Organized pony racing is a recent innovation in the UK: the first regulated pony race (using rules based on Arabian racing – see below) took place at Newton Abbot racecourse in 2004, and the current regulatory body, the Pony Racing Authority (PRA), was formed in 2007. The PRA works closely with the Pony Club, the BHA, the British Racing School and the PPA to introduce youngsters aged from nine to fifteen to the principles of race-riding, and it organizes series of racing at certain point-to-point and professional racecourses.

Young riders going for it in the closing stages of a pony race. (Photo: Nigel Kirby, for PRA)

Where they appear, the usual form is for a couple of pony races to be run before the main adult races, and the races are typically divided by pony size and rider age (which ranges from nine to fifteen), although there is some overlap on the latter. Distances vary from sprint distances (5 and 6 furlongs) up to 1 mile 2 furlongs, although most are shorter than the latter.

The work of the PRA has been remarkably successful in that it has introduced a large number of children from a variety of backgrounds to race-riding, not only in the amateur sport of point-to-pointing, but also to riding professionally. A number of young professional jockeys, now riding for top trainers, came into the sport via pony racing. If there are any pony races scheduled on a day when you visit a course, it is well worth getting there in time to watch them – you just might see a future top jockey.

Arabian Racing

Arabian horses, as mentioned in Chapter 1, had a major impact on the development of the Thoroughbred, and the breed continues to be highly regarded in many parts of the world. Arabian racing is, in fact, a major equestrian sport in more than thirty countries including states in the Middle East, Russia and France, who come under the umbrella of the International Federation of Arabian Horse Racing (IFAHR). In the UK, this form of racing was initially promoted in the 1970s by the Arab Horse Society with support from the Jockey Club but, since the turn of this century, the governing body has been the Arabian Racing Organisation (ARO), which operates with the support of the BHA.

Arabian racing action. (Photo: Shutterstock)

Arabian racing in the UK takes place on racecourses used for Thoroughbred racing under rules very similar to BHA rules. Whereas, in many other countries, the races for Arabians are part of a mixed card (i.e. some races are for Arabians, while some are for Thoroughbreds), in most cases in the UK, the meetings are all-Arabian affairs.

The Arabian racing season starts in spring and runs through until autumn. Admission charges are generally lower than for Thoroughbred racing, children may get in free and parking is usually free. There is a positive attitude towards welcoming and accommodating disabled spectators.

Arabian racing is quite 'democratic' in terms of the human involvement. While some of the keenest adherents, promoters and supporters are very wealthy Sheikhs, Arabian racing also offers opportunities for enthusiastic owners, who may perhaps breed and then also train and ride their own horses, to compete against expensive, professionally trained opposition.

In the UK Arabian races are open to amateur riders (although IFAHR rules allow professional jockeys to be booked for some of the top-level races). All jockeys must be licensed (there are various criteria to confirm competence) and the minimum age at which riders can apply for a licence is sixteen.

So far as the horses are concerned, Arabians are smaller than Thoroughbreds, and not as fast, but they can still go a good gallop. Unlike Thoroughbreds, who often start racing at two, Arabians in the UK don't start until three and all their races are on the flat but, these differences aside, there are a lot of similarities. The span of race distances is very similar to Thoroughbred racing, as are the broad categories of race types – handicaps, age- and sex-specific, level weights, etc. As with Thoroughbred racing, the top level are group races and one little quirk is that, whereas most Arabian races are started from a barrier like NH races, the group races use starting stalls. It is possible to bet on Arabian racing, with a small number of bookmakers available at ARO meetings and, for those interested in studying form, some information is given on the racecards and more is available from the ARO website and other specialist sites.

Arabian racing offers an entertaining, relatively inexpensive day out for the whole family and is also well worth a visit out of interest from more regular attendees of the Thoroughbred forms.

CHAPTER 3

The People Who Make Racing Happen

In explaining something of racing's history and the types of racing available, the previous chapters touched on the development and functions of racing's organizing authorities at national level who, obviously, are ultimately in charge of administering, regulating and promoting the sport. This chapter explains the roles of other people who contribute to delivery of the sport in various ways.

RACEHORSE OWNERS

It is self-evident that, if no one owned racehorses and paid all the costs associated with their upkeep, training, healthcare, entry fees, etc. there would be no racing, and thus no employment for trainers, jockeys, stable staff, racecourse staff and the many other people involved in the delivery of the sport. Buying, owning and racing horses is an expensive undertaking, but one of the fascinations of the sport is that it is not just the mega-wealthy who reap the rewards of doing so. Although any individual who owns just one or two horses can be considered pretty 'well off' by average standards, there is widespread approval when such an individual's horse wins a major race, and the same applies when a 'one-horse' syndicate of like-minded enthusiasts pulls this off. In addition, there have, for some years, been owners' clubs, whereby people on modest incomes can buy a small share in a horse and, on occasion, cheer 'their' horse on to victory. The other side of the coin – most welcome in my opinion – is the attitude and involvement of some of the owners who are mega-wealthy. It is easy to think of race-horses as 'rich people's playthings' (and there may well be some examples), but it is very evident that some prominent multi-horse owners absolutely love the sport and their horses, and make a huge contribution to racing.

To move on to a less pleasant topic, there has long been a general view that, when horses retire from racing, they are habitually abandoned or sold for meat. While it is true that there have, on occasion, been disgraceful incidents of abandonment, the 'norm' is that owners will, if they have the facility, look after their own horses in retirement, or otherwise take steps to find them a new home where they may be retrained for other equestrian roles: a lot of ex-racehorses, hunt, point-to-point, event, showjump, do dressage, enter showing classes (some of which are framed specifically for them) or simply become hacks. In addition to private arrangements along these lines, there are now a

Retraining of Racehorses Charity

Launched in 2000, this is British Horseracing's official charity concerned with the welfare of horses who have retired from racing. It raises funds from within the industry, promotes the potential of former racehorses to adapt to other activities, runs and funds a programme of educational clinics and competitions, and provides information and assistance to owners and trainers in respect of rehoming.

number of charities that specialize in retraining and rehoming racehorses. One of the displays that can sometimes be seen nowadays on big race days is a parade of former racehorses, sometimes being ridden in the manner of their current employment.

TRAINERS AND THEIR STAFF

People who have had 'B' movie crime capers or TV detective series inflicted upon them may have been given the impression that anyone can keep a racehorse in a garden shed, fed on a diet of carrots and sugar lumps and, in due course, turn up to the local racecourse to have him ridden to victory in the season's big race by a random teenager.

Racecourses often have attractions additional to the actual races. Here, at Sandown's parade of champions, former top-classes horses are paraded before an admiring crowd. A similar feature, seen increasingly frequently, is a parade by retired horses who have retrained into new roles.

In real life, things just don't happen like that. All trainers and jockeys involved in racing run by the BHA are subject to strict licensing procedures and must comply with a large number of ongoing rules and regulations.

It is possible for an individual to get a full licence to train flat horses, jumpers, or both. In the realm of NH racing, there is also a permit holder's arrangement, whereby someone can be licensed to train just horses owned by themselves or people who are, in simple terms, family members. While some big trainers, particularly those associated with flat racing, may train a couple of hundred horses, permit holders understandably tend to have quite small yards, but may do pretty well with the horses in their charge.

In addition to meeting the criteria necessary to acquire a licence to train (which has to be renewed annually), trainers are required to comply with a number of regulations relating to factors such as care and management of horses in training, compliance with the rules of racing, compliance with employment law and public liability requirements, etc.

Running a training yard is a business involving many different functions carried out by a number of staff. Some secretarial/administrative roles mimic those common to many businesses, such as administering employment records, the staff payroll, the payment of suppliers, invoicing clients (owners) and dealing with VAT returns, but also include functions specific to training horses, such as maintaining horses' medical and shoeing records, keeping stock records of feed and bedding and, very importantly, ensuring that horses are entered on time for those races at which they have been tar-geted. Although many of these tasks are, essentially, 'office jobs' they often attract people who have a great love of horses, and it is quite common for various members of a trainer's 'office staff' also to be involved in exercising some of the yards' equine inhabitants.

In addition to the mainly administrative staff, there are other important supporting roles, such as assistant trainer (frequently someone gaining experience with a view to running their own yard in future), the 'head lad' (who won't necessarily be a lad by either age or gender), who acts as team leader for the stable staff and is likely to be in charge of feeding the horses and administering medication under veterinary direction, and the travelling head lad/box driver (who may be two different people or the same one), with the responsibility for delivering runners (and all necessary kit) to the races in good time and good mental and physical state, regardless of roadworks and weather conditions. There will also be back-up from a specialist equine veterinary practice and a highly accomplished farrier.

The staff at the sharp end are those who look after and exercise the horses full time, and typically travel with their individual charges to race meetings. In recent years, there has rightly been an industry-wide increase in expressions of appreciation for these hardworking individuals. Working effectively in a racing yard requires not only a great affinity with horses and a range of practical skills, but also acute powers of observation and a very conscientious approach. The ability to sense a slight inconsistency of movement in a horse at exercise, a slight change of demeanour in the stable, or to feel the merest hint of heat in a limb – and then to report such concerns promptly and as precisely as possible – are all actions that could prevent or minimize problems that might otherwise interrupt a whole season or even compromise a horse's career. It is no surprise that people who have both the skill and attitude to do this type of work well, develop very close relationships with the horses in their care and take what amounts to a proprietorial interest in them.

JOCKEYS

The minimum age at which anyone can start race-riding under BHA rules nowadays is sixteen, but there are ways in which youngsters can hone their riding skills earlier than this, for instance by taking part in other mounted events from a young age, including official pony racing (*see* Chapter 2). Also, the children of trainers (or friends/associates/employees of trainers) may start riding out racehorses (exercising them at home) before the age at which they are permitted to race-ride, if they have developed sufficient skill and strength to do so.

Two organizations that have been hugely beneficial to aspiring jockeys in recent years are the British Racing School, founded in 1983 and based in Newmarket; and the Northern Racing College, founded in 1984 and based near Doncaster. The original focus of these charitable bodies was on training individuals who had the potential to ride as professional jockeys but, while this remains a major aim, they have branched out to provide courses for young adults interested in a variety of careers within the racing industry.

In order to apply for an initial jockey's licence (as an apprentice, on the flat or a conditional in NH races) the applicant must be over sixteen but under twenty-six years old, and employed by a licensed trainer (in a capacity other than actually race-riding), who supports the application. There are a number of criteria relating to health, competence, character, etc. that must be met in order for the application to be successful.

Once a licence has been granted, the individual can begin riding in races. This will initially be for the employing trainer but, if a young jockey shows promise, this may attract the attention of other trainers, who may offer 'outside' rides, subject to the agreement of the jockey's employer.

To compensate for lack of race-riding experience, apprentice and conditional jockeys are given a weight allowance, which is deducted from the weight a horse they ride actually carries when they are riding against full professional jockeys (so if the horse is allotted 9st 5lb and the rider is allowed 5lb, the horse carries 9st). The allowances reduce as the jockey rides more winners, as follows:

Apprentices on the flat
7lb until they've ridden 20 winners
5lb until they're ridden 50 winners
3lb until they've ridden 90 winners

Conditionals in NH races
7lb until they've ridden 20 winners
5lb until they've ridden 40 winners
3lb until they've ridden 75 winners
A conditional jockey can claim an additional 3lb when riding for their employing trainer in certain races, if they have ridden fewer than five winners.

In some high-value races, although they may be permitted to ride, riders who would otherwise claim an allowance are not permitted to claim it, so the obvious reason for trainers using them is negated. However, on occasion, a trainer may still use a claiming rider in such a race. This can be a mark of the trainer's confidence that the claimer gets on particularly well with the horse, and it is not unusual for such trust to be rewarded.

If this happens to a claimer with any degree of regularity, it is a sign that they are likely to have a successful career when they lose their claim.

Once jockeys have 'ridden out their claim' (become full professionals), they may either be retained by a trainer (have some form of contract to ride the horses from that yard) or become freelance. Many jockeys nowadays have an agent (*see* below) to help them book rides, and a few high-profile jockeys have arrangements to ride all a wealthy owner's horses (which may be with more than one trainer). Other than any retainer they may have, jockeys are paid a set fee per ride, and also receive a set percentage of prize money.

In addition to riding in races, an important part of a jockey's job is 'riding work', which entails doing fast work at home on horses being prepared for races. The way in which they ride these horses, and their feedback on how the horses performed, is invaluable to the trainer. As part of this role at home, jump jockeys will also school horses over fences to improve their technique and versatility. With all this to do, it would be a pretty normal day for a jockey to ride two or three horses at a trainer's yard first thing, drive a couple of hours to a racecourse, then ride in maybe four races before going home. The fact that many of them seem able to do this day in, day out on a diet apparently consisting of a good breath of fresh air and a sideways glance at a salad is one of life's mysteries.

In addition to professional jockeys, there are a number of amateurs who race-ride. The majority of these nowadays ride over jumps, probably because there is the opportunity for them of a grounding in point-to-pointing, and perhaps because not so many people nowadays can naturally ride at the sort of weights required for the flat. As with professionals, amateurs also have to be licensed subject to assessment and compliance with various criteria, and they can apply for either a category A or B permit. The former can ride either on the flat or over fences, but only in races confined to amateurs. The latter can ride in the same races as category A amateurs, but also in other races except those specifically confined to professionals. It is noteworthy that, since 1980, three winners of the Grand National have been ridden by amateurs.

As with apprentice/conditional jockeys, amateurs are entitled to a reducing weight allowance until they have ridden a certain number of winners. This will usually be as follows, but may be subject to individual race conditions:

Amateurs in races against professionals in NH races
7lb until they've ridden 20 winners
5lb until they've ridden 40 winners
3lb until they've ridden 75 winners

Amateurs in NH races confined to amateurs
7lb until they've ridden 5 winners
5lb until they've ridden 10 winners
3lb until they've ridden 20 winners

Amateurs don't usually compete against professionals on the flat and, in the few amateur-only flat races, similar arrangements to NH races apply.

Many amateurs will ride their own, or family-owned horses, but highly proficient individuals may also get rides from other sources. Some riders who began their career as amateurs have gone on to be highly successful professionals.

Jockeys' Agents and Valets

Both these people play important supporting roles to jockeys, allowing them to focus more on their main job of race-riding, and both need to be licensed by the BHA (assistant valets need to have permits).

Although retained jockeys will take many of their rides for the trainer retaining them, they may also take rides for other trainers, and freelance jockeys may ride for a large number of different trainers. Booking rides to optimum effect can be a very complex business all round, made even more so by factors such as meetings being cancelled because of adverse weather, changing ground conditions causing horses to be withdrawn/re-routed, intended runners going lame a couple of days before a race, horses being entered at more than one meeting to allow for last-minute decision-making and a myriad other reasons. It therefore makes sense from a jockey's perspective to have a reliable person to cope with this 'admin' – and perhaps sometimes to keep a disappointed trainer at one remove! However, agents can also be useful to trainers in terms of ease of contact and, if the jockey they were hoping to book already has commitments, the agent may be able to suggest another of his clients who is free, or already going to the course in question for a couple of rides and thus available, as an alternative.

It may be a little frivolous to describe valets as surrogate mums to jockeys, or the equivalent of 'dressers' in the theatre, but it may not be far from the truth – although, in practice, their role is pretty important. As we've seen, jockeys have busy lifestyles with riding work at first light, driving around the country from one meeting to the next and riding in as many races as practical. This leaves little time for issues such as cleaning clothing and ensuring that equipment is in good order. For this reason, jockeys employ valets as laundrymen, boot polishers, silks sorter-outers, saddle and weight-cloth checkers, borrowers of forgotten kit and general organizers, in the hope that they then won't go to weigh out carrying the wrong saddle, or walk into the paddock wearing odd boots and the wrong silks. Bearing in mind that a valet will typically have a number of client jockeys, this can be an exercise in logistics on a busy day. However, this may be a case of the boot being (figuratively, one hopes) on the other foot, because quite a few valets are themselves ex-jockeys, so they understand the need to attend to a lot of details in a short time whilst also wondering what to tell the connections of their forthcoming ride if he plays up at the start/won't settle/jumps with his eyes shut/would go faster on a carousel.

After the final race the valet, having consoled one of his clients who was beaten by a head in the big race, will gather up all the muddy gear and head off for a heavy evening's cleaning, often followed by an early morning's start next day to head off to a new meeting several hours' drive away.

BOOKMAKERS

The idea that bookmakers contribute to racing might seem, at first glance, rather odd. The common perception is that it is simply a vehicle by which they make money from people backing the wrong horse. In reality, they make a very considerable contribution to the sport.

The most obvious contribution is that, under the government's Horserace Betting

Levy regulations, they are obliged to contribute a proportion of their profits from betting on horseracing to the Levy Board (a non-departmental public body sponsored by the Department for Culture, Media and Sport). The largest share of this levy goes towards racing prize money, while the rest goes to provide funding for racecourse and integrity services, training and education, veterinary science, breeding improvement and loans to courses for capital projects.

While this contribution does, in a way, provide some benefit to bookmakers insofar as it helps promote competitive racing and possibly attracts more race-goers, it might be stretching a point to suggest that it results from anything other than a statutory demand upon them. However, another contribution that is both voluntary and beneficial to racing (albeit that it helps to advertise their business) is the degree to which bookmakers sponsor races. (There are certain constraints surrounding this, but it is quite prevalent.) Increasing prize money is clearly of benefit to horses' connections and riders, and tends to attract large, competitive fields, which in turn are attractive to race-goers and increase gate money. Of course, races of this sort can be quite a challenge when it comes to picking winners, so the bookies* are likely to get some of their sponsorship back in the form of losing bets – an example of the circle of life.

RACECOURSE STAFF AND OFFICIALS

Individual racecourses are in various ownerships. As mentioned in Chapter 1, a number are owned by the Jockey Club; others are owned, either as part of a group or individually, by companies that run them as businesses, often using them for various other functions on non-racing days. As companies, they have structures broadly similar to other commercial operations in terms of directorships and managerial roles focusing on marketing, customer liaison, hospitality, regulatory compliance and so on. Clearly, in order to function efficiently and deliver their key 'product' attractively, it is necessary that all their staff exhibit high levels of professional competence but, for the purposes of this chapter, I intend to concentrate on those whose roles are closest to the actual racing.

Stewards

The stewards are the people responsible for ensuring that all aspects of a race meeting are conducted under the rules and procedures laid down by the BHA. All stewards have to be approved by the BHA but, for most people, the role is an honorary one – the exception being the stipendiary stewards (commonly two per meeting) who are salaried employees of the BHA. The stewards are supported in their work by a stewards' secretary.

Although their potential roles and functions are many and varied, stewards are perhaps best known to the public for carrying out post-race enquiries when there has

---

* As bookmakers are commonly known. Both terms are used within this text.

been an objection (either by themselves or other interested parties) to the initial result of a race, or when there are concerns about some other incident that may have involved an infringement of the rules. They have wide-ranging powers to impose penalties for rule infringement and can refer more serious breaches on to the BHA.

Clerk of the Course

This official may sometimes have an additional title, such as Head of Racing. The most significant role of this post is maintaining the course in the best possible racing condition, a task that, in the longer term, may require involvement in major projects such as renewing drainage and watering systems, returfing, etc. In the lead-up to a meeting the clerk's role will also involve making judgements on the basis of weather forecasts about whether the course might, for instance, require additional watering to make the ground safe for racing, or the railing off of sections of the track to keep a strip of fresh ground available for the latter days of an extended meeting. In fairly recent years, owing to the availability of large sections of protective covering, it has become an option for clerks of some courses to make a decision as to whether this material should be laid to protect large sections of the course (usually a jumping course) from frost penetration, which would previously have rendered the ground unraceable. It still remains the clerk's ultimate responsibility to decide whether a meeting can go ahead or not, and to ensure that this decision is relayed to all interested parties as soon as practicable. In the execution of his various duties, the clerk will work with a team of support staff.

It's not all glamour – ground staff replacing divots on a wet day in February.

Stable Manager

This post is a requirement of the BHA, and the individual concerned must be vetted by that body prior to appointment. The stable manager is responsible for accommodating all the horses who have travelled to the course, whether for an overnight stay (as is sometimes the case with horses travelling a long distance) or on the day of the race, as well as catering for the requirements of their attendants, which, again, may include overnight accommodation. Maintaining a high level of security is an important part of the stable manager's role, as is ensuring stable hygiene – the transfer of infectious diseases between horses in a racecourse stables could potentially have a serious impact on a large number of training establishments. The stables themselves and the horsebox park also have to be maintained to the standards designated by the BHA.

Vet

Veterinary support at all race meetings is mandatory under BHA rules and there must be a minimum of two vets (three, for jump meetings) in attendance at any meeting before racing begins. There must also be a horse ambulance and a recovery vehicle with staff available. One of the key aims of these arrangements is to ensure that any horse injured during a race receives veterinary attention as quickly as possible and that, if appropriate, he can be transported to a veterinary hospital. Also, a racecourse vet will examine any horse who has got loose and galloped around prior to the start of a race to see whether he is in a fit condition to participate, may examine any horse about whose performance in the race the trainer expresses concern, and treat minor injuries such as cuts that a horse has incurred mid-race. A vet attending at the start of a race will be able to assess any concerns about a horse's soundness or action that his jockey may have raised on the way to the start, and check any horse who has been inadvertently kicked by another runner, or who (in a flat race) may have hurt himself in the stalls. He may also assist the farrier with reshoeing a horse and check that the horse is sound following this procedure.

Farrier

A farrier will be present at all meetings. Overall, his job is to assist with any hoof-related emergencies, but his most common role, as suggested above, is to deal with shoeing problems that most commonly surface after horses have cantered to the start of a race. The shoes fitted to horses for racing are lightweight and fairly flimsy compared to standard horseshoes, and it is not unknown for a shoe to become loose, or even lost, on the way to the start. In the event of this happening, connections have the choice of the horse being either withdrawn or reshod. If the latter option is taken, the farrier will undertake the task there and then. It is fascinating how quickly and expertly this can be done, and also how amenable most race-ready Thoroughbreds are to the process.

Since any significant delay to the start of a race can impact on the smooth running of a meeting, it makes sense for the farrier to be present at the start of any race and it is a BHA requirement that this is so for major races. If, for any reason, the farrier is not available at the start when needed, there is an option for the vet to remove a damaged shoe, but not (by law) to reshoe the horse unless he also happens to be a qualified farrier.

Medical Staff

In addition to providing veterinary care for horses, racecourses also have in place measures to deal with human medical concerns (for instance, racing cannot take place unless there are two ambulances present). These measures are aimed primarily at jockeys, but it is worth noting that BHA guidance stipulates that: 'Medical Staff present on licensed racecourses and point-to-point courses are there to deliver appropriate clinical care to any individual presenting with an acute medical problem as guided by the GMC "Duties of a Doctor".' Further to this, courses will have a first aid facility available to anyone taken ill whilst attending a meeting.

The BHA centrally is responsible for standards of medical care for jockeys, and the relevant practices and procedures are co-ordinated by the Chief Medical Adviser. All racecourse doctors, along with other attending medical staff, will be on the BHA's register of approved medical staff, and will be headed by a senior racecourse medical officer.

The BHA's procedures include monitoring the progress of injured jockeys to ensure that they only return to race-riding once it is safe for them to do so. A database of all jockeys' injuries is accessible to all racecourse doctors and one of their roles is to ensure that any jockey returning from injury is, in fact, fit to return to the saddle. Similarly, they will assess any jockey who has had a fall to check whether he is fit to take further rides that day, and treat any other instances of injury or health concerns. It is the course doctor who has the final say on whether a jockey is fit to continue riding and, in some instances, such as cases of concussion, a jockey will be 'stood down' for a statutory period.

Clerk of the Scales

The clerk of the scales is responsible for ensuring, firstly, that the horse a jockey is due to ride has been properly declared and is eligible to run, and that the jockey is eligible to ride; secondly that the jockey is wearing the correct colours and carrying any headgear (blinkers, etc. – although these aren't included in the weighing process) that the horse has been declared to wear in the race; and thirdly that every jockey carries the correct weight when riding in a race. In the interests of time efficiency, jockeys usually 'try' their weight on another set of scales before visiting the clerk and, if necessary, add such weight as they think is needed in the form of flat lead weights to their weight cloth, which will be fitted under the saddle. However, the clerk is the official arbiter of whether the jockey's weight is correct so, if the jockey initially weighs light, this must be amended before he can 'pass the scales'. If a jockey (and his relevant equipment) weighs above the allotted amount, it may be possible to amend this by, for instance, using a lighter saddle but, if this is not practical, the amount of overweight will be announced to the public. However, no jockey is allowed to weight out at 4lb or more above the allotted weight.

After the race, the jockeys of the first four horses (and, if there is prize money for more than four places, the other relevant jockeys) must weigh in (pass the scales again), as must any other jockey required to do so by the stewards. If a rider weighs in at 2lb or more over the weight at which he weighed out, the clerk must report him to the stewards (a minor increase could be explained by matters such as rain-soaked or mud-splattered clothing), and he must also do this if a jockey weighs in at 1lb or more less than he weighed out. (Again, there could be a legitimate reason for a very minor loss of weight, such as excessive sweating caused by a hard ride on a hot day, but an objection to an underweight of 1lb or more will result in disqualification.) If a jockey whose finishing position requires him to do so fails to weigh in, his horse will be disqualified. (This does happen, very occasionally, apparently as a result of those 'brain fade' moments that can affect most human beings.)

Commentator

All racecourses employ a commentator to cover the time from when the runners leave the paddock through until when the race is over. Television channels often have their own commentator, but sometimes they relay the course commentary.

A commentator's early observations on the way in which horses behave when leaving the paddock and on the way to the start can be useful for people who are perhaps considering a last-minute bet on a horse with a reputation for getting over-excited before a race. Commentating on the actual races is a highly skilled process, especially when there are big fields, particularly over shorter distances. Apart from their skill in race-reading, commentators usually have a vantage point that gives them a better overall view than most race-watchers, and they may have the luxury of additional feeds to monitors. Even when watching your fancy closely, it is useful to listen to the commentary on a race, since it will almost certainly add details of which you are unaware.

Starter

Starting a race is a highly responsible role – the starter has responsibilities to the racing authorities (any race that starts even fractionally before the official start time will be declared void), to the horses' connections and to the betting public. He must ensure that all the horses are fit to race and ready to start and that, so far as is practical, all the runners set off on level terms. If he believes that there has been a false start, he must make this immediately plain to the jockeys and the flag man (see below), who will act to prevent the field from going too far.

On the flat, the starter is responsible for ensuring that the horses are installed in a stipulated sequence, which is: horses who were blindfolded on their previous run (or for whom a blindfold has been requested for this run); horses with odd-number draws; horses with even number draws. However, there are various exceptions permitted and the starter also has discretion to vary the prescribed order 'in the interests of speedy and efficient loading' – all of which has the potential to present him with something of a conundrum. Even when the horses are all installed, the starter still needs to be alert to any last-minute problem, such as a horse rearing and/or getting a foreleg over the front of the stalls, or a panicky horse bursting out through the front of his stall (difficult, but technically possible as a safety measure). Although it happens very rarely, there have also been isolated incidents of a stalls malfunction where, for example, only some of the stalls open. In such cases, very prompt action is necessary on the part of the starter and his team.

Starters of NH races face different challenges, the primary one being the manner in which these races are started. Instead of stalls, the starting device is a fairly rudimentary barrier, which is positioned in front of the horses before the start and freed when the starter operates the starting mechanism. The standard method of starting a jumps race is for the field to be sent back some distance away from the start then, on the starter's instruction, to approach steadily. The starter, seeing that the runners are all together and in pretty close proximity, will then raise the barrier, allowing horses on their way. I've used the term 'pretty close proximity' here because, unlike flat racing, in which it is considered important that all horses start off in a level line, this is less the case with races over jumps. Although no one – starter, stewards, punters or connections – wants to see patently ragged starts, it is a fact that NH races generally take place over consider-ably longer distances than flat races and it is accepted that, for perfectly good tactical reasons, some jockeys will not want their mounts to be prominent in the early stages, and will thus be happy to give away a little ground at the start. (A similar thing happens in longer distance races in human athletics.) However, in case any horse is actually reluc-tant to start (**dwells** or **plants**), the starter's assistant will often follow in behind the runners as they approach the start ready, if necessary, to crack a whip behind them to encourage them forward. This is not used to actually hit any horse and in most cases no such action is needed.

A problem that can arise is that nowadays there is a stipulation that the horses should approach the starting barrier no faster than trot – which is fine if that is adhered to. However, this is easier said than done if one or two horses (or jockeys) get over-excited on the approach and these horses become keener and keener to break into a canter or gallop. Although their jockeys *should* be able to control them, this can be difficult, espe-cially if the approach began an unnecessarily long way from the start (as sometimes happens) and/or is downhill. Since horses are herd animals, once a couple are trying hard to speed up, the others will be incentivized to do so as well, and this can result in several of the field approaching the start faster than regulations permit. If this happens, the starter is (quite rightly) not allowed to let the race commence, but must abandon the start and reconvene it, this time with the runners stationary immediately in front of the starting barrier. This fairly recent innovation can, however, be a further cause of unsatisfactory starts. Once a field of race-ready horses has been geed up, it is difficult to keep them quiet and still – the adrenalin in their systems will make them likely to fidget in various ways, turning sideways, backing up and so on – sometimes even getting tangled in the barrier. Furthermore, there will be jockeys trying to re-establish their desired position – although there is no draw for NH races, jockeys may have their own preference about where they wish to be, and will try to get back there if they can. As a result, these stationary starts often involve a good deal of milling about and there is a risk that, despite the starter's best efforts, when he lets the field go, at least one runner will, in some way, be disadvantaged by the supposedly 'level' start.

Starter's Assistant

Key roles of this official are to check that all the runners are down at the start and, on the flat, to remind jockeys of their draw number. Another role (which may also involve help from stalls handlers) is to assist the jockeys in last-minute checks to their saddlery. By the time horses have cantered to the start it will be necessary to have their girths (the strap that holds the saddle in place) checked. Most horses, in all forms of equitation, will tend to 'tighten up' around their mid-section after they've been ridden for a few minutes and this is particularly true of race-fit athletes who have just had a significant canter and whose systems are primed to 'go'. Even with these checks, it is not unknown for a horse's saddle to slip back during a race, making the jockey's position precarious and the task of trying to ride an effective race very difficult, so all concerned are at pains to try to prevent this from happening. At this stage of girth-checking, the starter's assistant may also help a jockey who has asked for any other item of equipment to be checked and readjusted, as necessary.

Stalls Handlers

Starting stalls are (with very rare exceptions in special circumstances) used in all races on the flat and, despite the education at home provided by all trainers, the way in which individual horses respond to them varies enormously. Many go in without any fuss at all, and stand quietly awaiting the start; others can be a bit edgy and a few are really difficult. The reasons behind horses' reactions to the stalls may be various and sometimes difficult for even their trainers to fathom, but could range from genuine suspicion/mistrust through low-level awkwardness on to outright stroppiness. Before judging them too harshly, we should remind ourselves that, in various circumstances, we human beings can exhibit the same characteristics, often whilst loudly asserting a rationale for our behaviour!

Stalls handlers are teams of experienced people, many of whom also work in other branches of racing, whose job it is to get horses into the starting stalls as quickly, calmly and efficiently as possible and, if a horse becomes upset once in the stalls, to do their best to calm him down. To achieve all of this, they work in teams under the instructions of the starter, using various methods appropriate to individual horses. Despite their own experience they may, on occasion, be assisted by individuals who have specialized skills in handling problem horses.

Two pieces of equipment commonly used to help install reluctant horses are blindfolds and blankets. Blindfolds are used for horses who are visually aware of where the stalls are located, and are reluctant to approach them; putting on a blindfold and leading the horse around briefly in different directions will both calm and confuse him, and it is then usually fairly easy to lead him into his stall. The blindfold has a quick-release fastening behind the horse's head and the jockey will remove it swiftly when the starter calls 'jockeys' before pressing the starting mechanism.

For safety's sake (to make it hard for a horse to go down in the stalls) the individual stalls are pretty narrow and some horses dislike the sensation of the sides of the stall against their own flanks and either get upset by this and/or are reluctant to enter the stalls. For such horses, specially designed blankets can be fitted to alleviate this sensation. Horses are rarely worried by the blankets themselves, since they are used to being rugged in their stables, or whilst travelling. Once the horse is installed, fastenings on the blanket are clipped to the stall and, when the horse leaves the stall, this arrangement pulls the blanket free.

Horses Who Refuse to Load

Very occasionally, despite the handlers' best efforts, a horse may prove so difficult to load that the starter orders him to be taken away from the starting area. Keeping other runners waiting, who may have been installed for several minutes, is unfair to them and risks the possibility that previously calm horses may become upset in the stalls, with the possibility of a snowball effect developing, which could lead to injury. A horse withdrawn by the starter will, for betting purposes, be a non-runner. If a problem of this nature recurs with a particular horse, the racing authorities will require that he passes a stalls test (loading successfully in a non-racing scenario) and repeated problems in this area will result in a ban from racing. Although no stalls are involved, persistent failure to set off at the start of jumping races may also result in a ban.

Flag Man

The flag man, an employee of the racecourse, is often an unconsidered player in the pageant of racing but, when needed, he plays a key and quite intrepid role. Before the starter lets the field go, the flag man stands, with his yellow flag, some distance down the course (before the first jump in a NH race, and 150 yards or so from the stalls in a flat race). If, for any reason, the starter declares a false start, it is the flag man's job to wave his flag vigorously as a visual aid to tell the jockeys to pull up. Assuming that there is no such problem, he will proceed with great dignity, to walk to the side of the course and duck under the rail. I have never seen a flag man run – they always conduct themselves like the old-time generals who led their troops from the front, and would march resolutely towards enemy fire with their sabre resting on their shoulder.

Judge and Photo Finish Operator

The judge is the official responsible for determining which horse has won the race, and which horses have been **placed**.* Although nowadays judges have hi-tech photographic equipment on hand to help them, this remains a highly responsible job – there have, in the past, been occasions when a judge has called a result incorrectly, giving rise to considerable mayhem.

The **photo finish** operator is responsible for setting up and operating the equipment that is used to produce the images that may be required to help the judge confirm the result of a very close finish. The correct operation of this equipment is crucial – imagine the fallout if it failed at a time when no one could be certain which horse had won the Derby, or the Grand National! This equipment is, nowadays, also used to supply information that is the basis for computing the finishing margins between all the horses in a race.

---

* This term is commonly thought of as meaning first, second or third, but can be subject to rather different interpretations, depending on the number of runners in a race, and whether it is applied purely in terms of finishing position or whether the focus is on betting. There is a fuller discussion in the panel 'Placed' and Place Odds in Chapter 6.

CHAPTER 4

Going to the Races

CHOOSING WHERE TO GO

Realistically, someone who decides to experience a day at the races is likely to have their choice of venue dictated by pretty pragmatic considerations – ease of travel, convenient time, additional attractions (after-race concert, friend's birthday outing, etc.) and perhaps quality of racing. In most cases, therefore, first trips will probably be to courses fairly close to home (primarily for that reason) unless, perhaps, a decision is made to go racing whilst on holiday.

While there will always be obvious reasons for going to courses that can be reached easily and fairly cheaply, it is worth considering some factors that can make going further afield seem attractive – at least on the odd occasion.

ABOVE AND OPPOSITE: Panoramic views of, respectively, Epsom, Sandown and Cheltenham racecourses.

One of the great attractions of racing in the UK is the enormous variety of racecourses – something far less evident in many other countries. There are courses with long histories, courses with royal connections, courses in beautiful environments, courses in less attractive surroundings (which may, nevertheless, host some good racing), flat courses, undulating courses, left-handed and right-handed courses – even a couple of figure-of-eight courses – and Goodwood, the plan of which suggests it was laid out by someone following a trail of breadcrumbs whilst in the grip of hallucinogenics, which serves to add to the overall charm of this downland course.

The varying terrain of these courses can have a material effect on the chances of individual horses, as we shall explore further when discussing form, and qualities such as action and conformation.

All courses are 'graded' by the racing authorities, which means, in simple terms, that some will host better-quality races than others, in terms of the actual ability of the runners. This means, if you want to see the very best horses in action, they are most likely to be found at the highest-graded courses, which will often have the most expensive charges for entry. However, this does not necessarily mean that racing at the 'lesser' meetings will not be competitive and enjoyable – indeed, forward-thinking courses will try to attract good fields of runners by framing the entry conditions of their races adroitly. It is also the case that the quality of races will vary at all meetings – even the

The Breakfast With the Stars Day, held at Epsom in May, is an early morning chance to see potential runners at the following month's Derby meeting having a workout around the distinctive track. The two horses here are coming around Tattenham Corner – the background clearly shows the downhill gradient.

Runners at the Cheltenham Festival going to the start in front of packed stands. Some race-goers may wish to strike a balance between the excitement of attending top meetings and having a little more room to manoeuvre.

'big names', such as Ascot, Newmarket, York, Cheltenham, etc. will have lesser cards, most probably on weekdays and/or in the evenings. This variation in the importance of meetings is likely to have an impact on the cost of entry – this will be higher than usual on the 'top' days, but perhaps cheaper on days when the course is offering some form of promotion.

Generally speaking, it is more entertaining for spectators if there is a fair number of runners in each race and it is in the interests of any course to try to attract as many runners as possible, since this will generate more income from various sources, but there will be times when the fields are rather small. There can be various reasons for this, usually beyond the control of the course officials. A common one is extreme **going**, a product of Britain's idiosyncratic climate. In recent years, there have been major improvements to the drainage and watering systems of many courses, and innovations such as special covers, used particularly to protect the ground from frost at winter jumping courses. However, there are practical limits to what can be achieved, and still occasions when racing has to be abandoned. Short of this, there are still times when the going is so heavy that it will prove unsuitable for certain runners (who will thus be withdrawn) or, conversely, too firm, with the same result. Ironically, although all-weather tracks can function in virtually all UK conditions, severe weather may compromise the ability of some trainers to transport their charges to a meeting safely, so even these courses may, in a manner of speaking, be affected by the weather. If you fancy going racing at times

Open Days

Some race meetings are linked to open days, when training yards in the vicinity open their doors to visitors, show them around and parade their leading horses. These visits can be very informative, and give members of the public a chance to see racehorses at close quarters and learn more about training regimes. For anyone interested in what goes on behind the scenes, these days are well worth a visit.

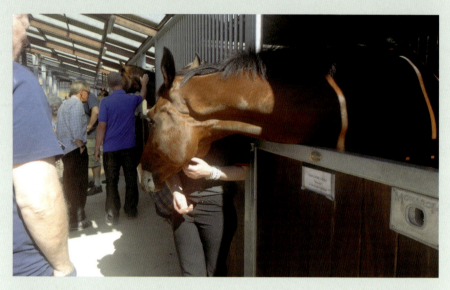

It can be fascinating to attend a stable's open day. Here, visitors are able to get up close and personal with some of their favourite horses.

Favourite horses are paraded at stable open days.

of extreme weather, it may be worth checking the likely runners the day beforehand, which can be done on websites such as racingpost.com or sportinglife.com. (One point to note is that races with fewer runners are not necessarily uninteresting – sometimes race conditions or circumstances can lead to a small field but, if the runners are high-class, the race can still be very exciting and/or illuminating.)

Regarding the type of racing you choose to watch, race-goers tend to divide into those who prefer flat racing, and those who prefer jumping. Some, however, enjoy both equally and anyone who fancies a 'taster' of both may like to attend one of the (relatively few) 'mixed cards', usually put on in spring, which feature both forms of racing at the same meeting. A further option is to attend either a point-to-point (amateur steeplechasing) or an Arabian race meeting, both of which were described more fully in Chapter 2.

POINTS TO CONSIDER

The following are just general notes for guidance. More details on the related issues may be available on the website of a course you are thinking of attending (as will a fixture list with times of first races, etc.).

Getting to the Course

I have already mentioned that newcomers to race-going are likely to make their first visits to fairly local courses, but it is still worth finding out something about the final stage of the journey in respect of ease of access. All courses, so far as I am aware, have parking facilities, but how easy it is to get into (and out of) them may be dictated to a considerable extent by the road layout of the surrounding area – and, although one possibility might be to park reasonably close to the course and then walk in, there may be parking restrictions in place to prevent clogging up of local residential streets. Parking within the racecourse area may sometimes be free in certain areas, or there may be a charge.

If you are thinking of having a few drinks as part of the day out it might, in any case, be worth considering other forms of transport. A number of courses are quite close to railway stations and some of those that are a little further away may organize a shuttle service from the station to the course. People living in the London area have a particularly attractive option available if they wish to visit Windsor racecourse – there are times when it is possible to alight at Windsor & Eton train station and take a riverboat for a short journey to the racecourse.

Categories of Entry

Racecourses have traditionally had various categories of entry with different prices, rather like concert halls, theatres, etc. These have names such as member's, grandstand and silver ring, but regardless of what a course actually calls these categories, they translate as posh seats, medium seats and cheap seats respectively. Which type you choose will depend entirely on personal requirements, and if you have any specific

Point-to-points

Because they are often run on land used mainly for other purposes, and rarely have solid structures, point-to-points may offer only limited shelter, probably in the form of the beer tent. This should be borne in mind if you are intending to take children or elderly people with you – and it's a particularly good idea to wear plenty of layers and a waterproof coat if you go to one on a sleety day in February. (*See also* Comfort and Convenience, below.)

ones it is worth checking the course website or ringing in advance to ensure that you go to the enclosure that suits you best. My own requirements are very basic – shelter available when necessary, access to the paddock and the facility to go out onto the course when appropriate, access to simple refreshments and reasonably sanitary toilets – but I appreciate that others may want to go a bit more upmarket.

Particularly for those who go for a more fancy option, perhaps intending to take in some fine dining, there may be a dress code involved, although this will not normally be anything like as formal as that applied to the Royal Enclosure at Ascot. Generally, something akin to 'smart casual' is fine, but if you intend to go relatively upmarket it may be worth checking the course website. The upside to getting dolled up is that, at some of the more major meetings, there are competitions for various 'best dressed' categories, if that's the sort of thing that floats your boat. (If, like me, you tend to go in the cheap seats, then pretty much anything that wouldn't get you arrested in public should be okay.)

There is extra pageantry on view at some major meetings, such as Royal Ascot.

Personal Requirements

Facilities relating to personal requirements may be, to some extent, tied into categories of entry.

Children are usually welcome at racecourses and there is often a concession on entry fees (in some cases, younger children may be admitted free). Some courses offer changing/feeding facilities, crèches and play areas. It is, of course, essential to keep a close eye on children in terms of safety. People taking teenagers racing should be mindful that the minimum legal age for betting is eighteen.

Access and facilities for disabled people, including those in wheelchairs is on the increase, and some courses allow guide dogs to accompany those who require them (although it is worth checking beforehand, since dogs are not usually allowed at professional racecourses, for fairly obvious reasons).

Trained medical staff are available at racecourses in the event that anyone is taken ill.

Catering All courses offer a range of food and drink; in some cases this will include fine dining options.

Financial services Some major meetings now have banking facilities available, and many have, at least, a cash machine. Note, however, that it is unwise to carry unnecessarily large amounts of cash at a race meeting, and sensible to take due care of wallets/card holders, as it would be in any busy public place.

Most courses offer a range of catering options.

Comfort and convenience I have already touched on dress codes, but it's worth making the point that a lot of people go racing in clothing that is not in their own best interests, especially if the intention is to get out there and really engage with the racing. We all know that the British weather is subject to what might be termed vagaries, so the sensible approach for anyone intending to spend half the day out of doors is one of well-honed cynicism.

(There used to be a TV weather forecaster who would give racing tips – that, surely, is the definition of irony: 'Can't tell for sure whether it will rain this afternoon, but here's my selection for the twenty-runner handicap.')

If you intend to spend some time walking down to watch starts, or horses jumping, remember that you will walking on quite long grass, which can get wet and be pretty muddy. (This applies even at all-weather courses, where it may be only the actual racing surface that is all-weather, and even this will get wet if it rains.) It will be evident that various types of footwear will be inappropriate for these conditions so, without necessarily going to full-on hiking boots extremes, it makes sense to put on footwear that won't leave you with trench foot and/or come off in the mud.

Another point is that racecourses are typically pretty wide open spaces and, although I've visited numerous winter meetings, it is easy to forget quite how cold it can be when a keen north-easterly is blowing freezing rain at you across what is essentially a big field. If you go racing in such conditions, remember that you can take a layer off, but you can't put it on if you haven't got it.

Regarding umbrellas (or parasols, if you've Continental genes and go racing in mid-summer), it's fine to take these, but please be careful not to put them up suddenly whilst

A good pair of binoculars is a great asset when race-going.

Racecard Information

Once you arrive at your chosen course you will find that, in addition to listing the day's races, the official racecard will include useful details relating to layout of the course and the available facilities. The racecard is discussed in detail in the next chapter.

in the vicinity of the horses. Another potential hazard to avoid is flash photography. The use of flash photography is rightly forbidden by racecourses and there may be restrictions on taking normal photos in certain areas, although in general, there is no prohibition on cameras as such. Another very useful item to take with you is a decent pair of binoculars, with which to follow the progress of your own fancy. They can also be used to mock your companions, by pointing your 'bins' back down the track as the winner comes home, and saying 'I still can't see yours.'

CHAPTER 5

Racecards and Their Interpretation

All race meetings sell racecards, which give information about the course, the facilities, the sponsors, etc. and details of each race. Generally speaking, they are becoming more detailed and informative these days – and more expensive in consequence – but they are worth having. Among other attributes, they include coloured images of the owners' colours, which help instant identification of horses either in the paddock or on course, and they are much smaller than newspapers and commonly printed on a relatively water-resistant surface, which means that, unlike newspapers, they are less prone to flapping around like a mad spectre when you are trying to read them in a stiff breeze or, in fact, dissolving into mush in a sudden rain squall when you are halfway through checking some key statistic. Another option is to look at the websites of the main racing journals on a tablet or mobile phone.

One of the limitations of racecards provided by courses is that they give only relatively little information about horses' past form. This, in fairness, is hardly surprising given the time constraints under which they are produced and the potential production costs (and thus sales price) that would be involved in trying to provide something more comprehensive. For those who want more detailed form statistics and professional comment on the runners, trainers, riders, etc., there are dedicated racing journals accessible online or available in hard copy either from newsagents or, frequently, from vendors at the course. On a more basic level, most daily newspapers cover race meetings on their sports pages, displaying the races in a layout that approximates to that of racecards and dedicated journals.

Many racecards provided by courses will include a basic guide explaining what the various figures and abbreviations mean but, while useful for a newcomer, there is little explanation of the potential significance of these ciphers. Appreciating such significance will make a racecard of much greater use when you are trying to decide which horse (if any) you wish to bet on. Since, as stated, there is no absolutely standard format for a racecard, whether between one course and another, or between different publications, I have constructed a sample of a 'typical' card (*see* below). The underlying key gives a very basic explanation of what the components mean, and it is followed by notes expanding on their significance. Text in italics indicates details likely to appear on racecourse cards, and probably in the form section of racing journals, but not usually in standard newspapers.

A SAMPLE RACECARD

3.30[1] LAME DUCK HANDICAP (5)[2] 3yo+(rated …)[3] £5,000 added (£2,800)[4] 1m 3f[5] (10)[6]

1.[7] (3)[8] 08/33-12[9] GISAPUSH[10] (24)[11] (H)[12] (CD)[13] (BF)[14] (G)[15] T. Rayner[16] 5-9-7[17]
G. Uppe (3)[18] (Rating)[19]
b g Too Weary–Shove Off[20]
Owner and Breeder[21]
Red, white stripes, blue sleeves and cap[22]

Other runners will be listed below the top horse in racecard numerical order.[23] Below the runners there is likely to be a betting forecast,[24] a pundit's view of the possible outcome[25] and possibly records of favourites in the race in the past few years,[26] ages of previous winners[27] and specific details of the most recent winner.[28]

Key
1. Time of the race.
2. Name, type and grade of the race.
3. Types of horses that may enter.
4. Total value of the prize money and amount to the winner.
5. Race distance.
6. Number of runners.
7. Racecard number.
8. Draw (relevant only to flat races).
9. Recent form figures.
10. Horse's name.
11. Days since previous run.
12. Additional equipment (here, H for hood).
13. Reference to horse's previous success in a race with some similarity to today's (here **CD** means course and distance winner).
14. **BF** means beaten **favourite** – the horse started favourite on his previous outing, but didn't win (finished 2nd, in this example).
15. Ground conditions considered to suit the horse – **G** here means good ground.
16. Name of trainer (*on course racecards, location of training establishment may be added*).
17. Horse's age and today's weight carried, in that order: here, five-year-old allotted 9st 7lb.
18. Name of jockey, and allowance, if any: here, jockey is allowed 3lb, meaning horse will actually carry 9st 4lb.
19. *On course racecards, the number here is likely to be the BHA official rating for the horse – i.e. the rating that will dictate his handicap mark. In other journals it may be a figure based on their racing correspondent's or other staff member's private assessment.*
20. *Colour, sex and parentage of the horse.* These details are likely to appear on course race cards; they are also available in the form section of dedicated racing journals.
21. *Again, owner's and breeder's details are likely to appear on course racecards;* they are also available in the form section of dedicated racing journals.

22. *This written description is likely to accompany an actual illustration on a course racecard.* Racing journals and (sometimes) regular newspapers will show the illustration only, just for major races.
23. How racecard order is established is explained in the following notes section.
24. The betting forecast is simply what some reasonably well-informed person involved in compiling the card thinks the runners' odds are likely to be. It is not definitive.
25. As with 24, this will be a potted comment by someone regarding their view of certain horses' prospects and the possible outcome.
26. Records of favourites in the last few years are, to my mind, of little significance (although *see* point 28 and following notes section).
27. Ages of previous winners can be significant, particularly where conditions races are concerned, as explained in the following notes section.
28. If a horse is entered in a race he won the previous year, this past performance means that his renewed presence is noteworthy – he is, at least, a course and distance winner. However, *see* the notes section for further discussion.

SIGNIFICANCE OF RACECARD FEATURES

1. **Time of the race** will be the precise time at which the race can be started, not the time when horses begin to assemble in the paddock.

2. **Name, type and grade of the race.** Many major races have a very long history; some will be sponsored and include the sponsor's name in the title; others can be obscure or wacky. Type and grade can be significant factors. For example, handicaps are graded such that the *higher* the number, the *lower* the grade. Thus if the race is a grade 2 handicap, and checking past form reveals that a horse you fancy has been running in grade 4 races, you should be aware that now (even though the weight he carries will take account of this step up in grade), he is basically racing against better horses. Similarly, in level weights and conditions races, it is worth comparing the grade(s) in which a horse has been racing previously with the grade of the current race – for example, a horse who has been getting placed in listed races is going to be a pretty long shot to compete in a grade 1 race.

3. **Types of horses that may enter** will deal with factors such as age, sex, past performance (for example, maiden races are not open to horses who have previously won under the relevant code) and, particularly in handicaps, current rating. (The eligibility for handicaps takes horses' official rating into account, so a handicap race will be open to runners within a certain ratings span.) In the case of some major races, such as the Grand National, there may be additional qualifying factors relating to type/distance of previous races won, etc.

4. **Total value of the prize money and amount to the winner.** These details are mainly of interest to connections who fancy their chances, but they also give an additional idea of the likely quality of the race.

5. **Race distance** is a key factor in assessing the chances of the runners – it is useful to

know which runners have previous good form over the same, or similar distances. *See also* point 13.

6. **Number of runners.** This is of interest in terms of each way and place betting (*see* Chapter 6) and, on this point, note that the number of runners on a racecard is the number declared to race at the time of publication. Horses may be withdrawn from a race for a number of reasons and any non-runners will be announced by the course as soon as officials are aware of this. However, the terms of each way and place betting relate to actual runners, not those on the racecard. Therefore, if you are thinking, for example, of backing a horse each way in the race that shows eight runners on the card, check that all eight are actually running because, if your fancy comes third and one runner was a late withdrawal, you won't be paid on third in a seven-runner field.

7. **Racecard number.** The horse at the top will be number 1. In a handicap (or some conditions races), this will be the top weight; in a level weights race, it will be the horse whose name is first alphabetically. The horses that follow will be numbered 2 upward, in handicaps, by sequence of weight carried (if two or more horses carry the same weight, they will be numbered in alphabetical sequence). In level weights races, the numbering will be strictly alphabetical. In conditions races entries will be numbered alphabetically by weight category – for example, those with 9st 7 A, B, C, etc., then those with 9st 4 A, B, C etc. If a number is omitted, this indicates that withdrawal of the horse concerned was notified in time for his details to be omitted from the card.

    If you intend to back a horse on a pool system, it is usual to give the racecard number and race time, rather than the horse's name, when you place your bet (*see also* Chapter 6 Betting).

8. **Draw (relevant only to flat races).** In flat races that are started from stalls (virtually all), there is a random draw for stall numbers carried out by Weatherbys* on the day that entries are declared (i.e. connections confirm their intention to run). The stalls are numbered sequentially from 1 up to the total number of horses in the race. Looking from behind the stalls, on tracks designated 'left-handed', the lowest number is to the left-hand side; on courses designated 'right-handed' the lowest number is on the right-hand side.

There are times when the draw can definitely have a significant influence on a horse's prospects. Unlike in human athletics, where shorter races have a staggered start (so that, in a 400m race for example, the runner on the inside of the track and the runner on the outside both actually run 400m), this does not occur in horse races. Therefore, particularly on tight, turning tracks, a horse **drawn wide** (i.e. with a high number) is at a disadvantage unless his jockey is able to make a swift manoeuvre towards the

---

*This is virtually always the case although there are rare exceptions. For the Stewards' Cup, a big sprint on the straight course at Goodwood, an invited celebrity effectively draws the entries 'out of a hat' in random order and the connections of the horse drawn can then choose which stall they want him to occupy. Responses seem to vary from a grateful, desperate grabbing of a fancied stall to a good deal of head-scratching.

Runners installed for a flat race: the numbers above the stalls show the draw.

inside. A similar point applies to relatively short races where the nature of the course is such that runners meet a bend only a furlong or so from the start – it also applies, to some extent, to sprints on those courses where the 'straight' actually contains a bit of a dogleg, meaning that a horse caught on the outside of the dogleg would travel slightly further than those on the inside.

Where a horse is drawn can also have an impact on other relevant factors. Although racecourse staff try very hard to produce going that is the same across the width of the track, on some courses, for various reasons related to subsoil, camber, etc., there may be a bias under some climatic conditions, which will either favour or disadvantage a runner, depending on where he is drawn. Where this is evidently the case, an astute jockey may be able to switch position from an unfavourable draw, although this will not be that easy, particularly in big fields over shorter distances and/or when other jockeys are trying to do something similar.

A more esoteric factor relating to the draw (which, again, is usually more relevant in big-field sprints) is where the 'pace' will be. This factor relates to the twin facts that some horses are happiest making the running (or being very prominent), whereas others relax and perform better if they can be **settled** in behind the front runners. The idea is thus that the latter will be assisted if they are drawn close to a horse or horses likely to make the running.

A final point about the draw is that, unless a horse is known to be difficult to load into the stalls, and is thus given an official dispensation to be loaded out of order, the draw numbers have an influence on whether a horse is loaded early or late, those with an odd number going in before those with an even number. The potential impact of this cannot be predicted prior to loading, but if there is some delay partway through the procedure, this is potentially disadvantageous to horses who have been in the stalls for some time, because even 'good loaders' have the potential to get restless in these circumstances while, conversely, there is the danger that others may 'switch off', leaving their jockeys with the dilemma of when to regain their attention without getting a premature response. There is more information about the loading process in At the Start in Chapter 7.

In terms of perusing racecourse cards, note that the draw number is not always positioned as in the example above, but may be, for instance, added after the weight carried. If betting on a pool system, ensure that you don't give the horse's draw number instead of his racecard number (if you do, unless they happen to coincide, you will back the wrong horse).

9. **Recent form figures.** These show, in numerical terms (and, where relevant, letters) the horse's previous performances, usually in his last six races. (If a horse is having his first race, no figures will be shown; if he has run fewer than six times, the figures shown will represent his races to date.) The figures run from left (sixth previous race) to right (most recent race). There are various conventions about how this form is shown:
   - A hyphen indicates a break between the previous season and the current one (thus 233-456 would show the last three runs of the previous season and the fact that the horse has run three times in the current season).
   - An oblique is used to show that there has been a whole season in which the horse didn't run (at least under the code of the current race), so 233/456 would indicate the last three runs of the season before last, a season's break, and three runs in the current season, while 23/3-456 would show two runs the season before last, just one run last season, and three runs in the current season. If a horse has been off the course for two whole seasons, some cards indicate this with a double oblique, as 233//456.
   - Certain letters are used to indicate that, for some reason, the horse didn't finish the race. These apply more usually (though not exclusively) to jump racing. Those in common use are:
   F = fell, which is self-explanatory.
   BD = brought down. The horse fell because he was knocked over/tripped up by another runner (usually one who had fallen just in front of him).
   U (sometimes **UR**) = unseated rider. This always means that the jockey parted company with the horse, but it covers everything from an inexperienced rider just falling off to circumstances where the horse, although not technically falling, made such a catastrophic blunder that the jockey would have had to defy the laws of gravity and physics to remain on board. It also covers situations such as a horse making heroic efforts to avoid another fallen runner that entailed rapid and unpredictable changes of momentum, balance and direction.
   R = refused. This, when seen, usually means that a horse refused a jump, which is rare in racing, but not unheard off. There can be different reasons behind it, such as an inexperienced horse 'putting the brakes on', a horse having 'run out of steam' (should probably have been pulled up – *see* below – before that fence), a horse suddenly feeling the effects of some injury on the final strides before an approach, or a horse being badly unsighted by some problem ahead. In a different context, it can sometimes refer to a horse failing to **'jump off'** at the start – i.e. refusing to race.
   RO = ran out. Means either that a horse avoided a fence by running round it (given the fact that both hurdles and steeplechase fences have 'wings' to guide

the runners, this is fairly uncommon, but not unknown), or he has run off the prescribed course, which can happen if a horse has very wayward tendencies or, for example, there has been a failure of equipment.

CO = carried out. Signifies similar consequences to ran out, but indicates that the horse and rider were victims of the actions of another horse. It might be, for instance, that a loose horse tried to avoid a fence or ran off the course, and took another horse with him. This is one reason why, in jumping races, jockeys try to remain acutely aware of the actions of a horse who is running free. Another reason why a horse might be carried out is if one more or less alongside suddenly sustains a serious injury and is incapable of maintaining a true line. Fortunately, this is a very rare occurrence: in most cases, if a jockey realizes that his mount has gone lame, he will try to ensure that he doesn't interfere with other runners in the act of pulling up (*see* below).

S (sometimes **SU**) = slipped up. This can happen if a horse loses his footing and balance, probably on a bend. While racecourse officials try very hard to ensure that the course is safe to race on, there are rare occasions when, perhaps because of an unforeseen change to climatic conditions, it becomes apparent that there may be an issue with a particular section of the track. In such circumstances, this will be investigated and, as necessary, there may be modifications to the course for the remainder of the meeting, or it may be abandoned.

P = pulled up.* The jockey has decided that the horse should not be asked to continue the race. There can be various reasons for this, the most serious of which would be that the jockey believes the horse has sustained an injury or physical impediment of some kind. The other main reason for this is that the horse has lost touch with the field, is getting tired and has no realistic chance of being involved in the finish. In such cases, it is prudent and humane for a jockey to pull up, because it is when horses get really tired that they are most likely to make jumping errors and become prey to various physical strains.

D = disqualified. Fundamentally, this means that, after the race, the stewards determined that the horse/jockey somehow infringed the rules of racing and the original placing did not stand. However, there are different circumstances in which this can happen, with different consequences and different ways of indicating them. The most serious scenario is that the horse was completely disqualified so that, in effect, his actual finishing position is of no consequence in terms of prize money, etc. For lesser transgressions, he might simply be demoted behind a placed rival whose chance he impeded in the closing stages of the race. For example, he finished first, a head in front of a rival, but the stewards judged that he would not have done so had he not interfered with that rival's progress. In such a case, the actual finishing order would be reversed. Where a horse has been completely disqualified, some racecards may supplement the D with a figure to show the horse's original finishing position, possibly as d1. Where the finishing order was reversed, a racecard is likely to show the horse's official position, rather than the finishing position.

---

* The term 'pulling up' is also commonly used to describe the actions of horses and jockeys after the finish of a race. Sometimes, if a horse has finished a race really full of running and is still 'tanking' after the winning line, a jockey may need to use overt pressure on the reins to slow him down. However, where practical, jockeys prefer to let their mounts ease down steadily, because this is physiologically preferable.

- Some publications use a mixture of plain and bold text to indicate form in different types of races. For flat racing, it is common to use plain text for turf and bold for all-weather form. (In this respect, it is worth remembering that horses can have different ratings between the two surfaces and some – though not all – horses perform better on one that the other.) For jump racing, it is common to use plain text for actual jumping and bold for NH flat races. (Some point-to-point racecards have a different convention, in that all form is shown in plain text, but form from past races under NH rules is set in brackets.)
- One crucial factor is how previous form is enumerated. In times past, it was general practice to use 1, 2, 3, 4 to indicate that a horse had finished first, second, third or fourth and, beyond this, to use 0 to indicate **unplaced**. However, this was of limited use because, without further information, 0 could mean anything from 'just out of the frame' to 'hopelessly tailed off' – imagine the difference between 0 representing a horse who finished sixth, two **lengths** behind the winner in a twenty-four runner race and one who finished nineteenth, beaten by twenty lengths. Nowadays, many racecards and journals use figures from 1 to 9 to indicate finishing positions, before reverting to 0 for tenth upward, so at least the race-goer knows that 0 has some degree of significance. (Further to this, one national newspaper at least uses the letter L to indicate that a horse finished last. I can only assume they think this is somehow helpful, but actually it seems pointless and misleading in the absence of any supplementary information. To see why (reasoning along similar lines to the changing meaning of 0, just mentioned), imagine the difference between a horse, raised in grade, who finished two lengths last of three whilst running perhaps his best race ever, and one who finished a tailed-off last of eighteen runners in a handicap. Furthermore, imagine a horse whose L signified being the last of six finishers in a gruelling staying steeplechase on heavy ground. Okay, he finished last, but perhaps there were a dozen other runners who either fell or pulled up, so his performance is considerably better than the L implies. My advice is to take little notice of this letter without having recourse to further information.

Of course, while the actual figures (and letters, where appropriate) give some basic clues to a horse's form, that is really all they do, and you shouldn't jump to conclusions based on these alone. There are, of course, warning signs that will rightly make you cautious about backing a horse. A jumper with more than an occasional F or U in his form is clearly a risky proposition (although some such horses can come up trumps when their jumping holds up) and I would always be wary about any horse who has shown a tendency to refuse to jump (without good reason) or to start **on terms** with the others (although there have been notable examples of horses with a reputation for being 'tricky' at the start showing considerable aptitude when they consented to do so). Also, while I have given reasons for horses being pulled up, I almost never back one who pulled up on his previous start, or has any record of doing so on a regular basis. In simple terms, if a horse cannot complete his races (for whatever reason), he doesn't seem to me a good betting proposition. Although this doesn't stop such horses winning on occasion, they don't do so under the burden of my money!

Regarding the form numbers, it is never a bad thing to see a good sprinkling of wins and places in the form – this is clear evidence, at least, that the horse has been able to feature prominently in his previous races. However, these figures still need to be viewed in context with the types of races he has been running in compared to the current race, and with the relative form of his current rivals. For example, a horse who has won his last three races in modest company may be totally outclassed if entered in a major conditions race, and the form figures 1212 attained by a horse in class 4 handicaps may not match the actual achievements of one whose figures 6564 were achieved in better-class races. Furthermore, a horse who has been winning and getting placed consistently in handicaps is likely to have his rating increased incrementally so that, as he continues to be successful, he will be allotted more weight. In many cases, the handicapper will 'catch up' with such a horse so that, although he may continue to run to his best, the weight differential with other horses will mean that he may struggle to replicate his form figures. Analysing these factors in any detail can really only be done through scrutiny of the form in dedicated racing journals, which is something you may wish to investigate as you become more engaged with the sport. The notes in these journals use symbols, etc. similar to those on racecards, and describe horses' performances in a kind of abbreviated English, which is not usually too hard to follow once you tune into it.

Finally, form figures should be viewed in conjunction with other information, as discussed in notes 13–15 below.

10. **Horse's name.** This is what you give if you are placing a bet with a course bookie ('£5 win Notahope') and it is the horse's names that the commentator will use when calling the race.

11. **Days since previous run.** This information can be useful, but it is easier to interpret its possible influence if you have access to the reason(s) behind it – which can be rather difficult unless there is some reference to it on the racecard, in a racing journal article and/or from an interview with a trainer. Horses, like human athletes, need to be brought steadily to peak fitness and, as with humans, an astute regime is necessary if they are to retain this level of fitness for an extended period of time. If there are any setbacks to their regime, it is likely that fitness levels will dip a little. Therefore, as a broad generalization, it is encouraging to see a horse whose recent form looks good (*see* point 9) appearing a relatively short time (let's say two to four weeks) after his previous race, since this suggests that the trainer is happy with him. However, if we accept this as broadly 'good', the consequent assumption is that a different scenario may be 'bad' or, at least, a concern. If it has been a very long time since a horse's previous race (*see* point 9) – and especially if the form of his last race suggests that he ran poorly – it is highly likely that the horse has been suffering from a significant physical problem. With the advance of veterinary procedures, access to facilities such as treadmills and swimming pools, and the advent of all-weather training surfaces, it is not so hard to bring a horse back from injury as was formerly the case – but it is still a major feat of horse management to bring a horse back from a long lay-off to run up to his full potential at the first time of asking. It can be done, but backing a horse after such a long lay-off is, at least, a considerable act of faith.

What about a horse simply having his first run of the season (*see* point 9)? It will, almost certainly, be a fairly long time since his previous race unless he is a dual-purpose horse who mixes flat racing and jumping. Some racecards cover this point by highlighting the fact that a horse may have had his most recent racecourse appearance under a different code from the current one. For example, if a hurdler had a race on the flat three weeks ago, this will be indicated by **(F21)**, which can be useful to know if his form figures suggest that this is his first (jumping) race of the season. The reverse may be also be true, so that a horse running on the flat would have the symbol **(J21)** – or whatever the number may be – to show he had his most recent race over jumps.

Again, it used to be the case that a seasonal first run was more significant than it is now – this applied particularly to the early spring of the flat season, if a cold winter had meant that the old grass gallops were intermittently unusable because of ice or frost. Nowadays, all-weather gallops pretty much avoid this issue, although it is still the case, with horses being living individuals, that some don't really thrive through the cold weather and need a degree of spring sunshine to help them to their peak. In this respect, the geographical location of some training yards can still be a factor and trainers will sometimes admit that their charges have yet to find their form. Therefore, particularly early in a season, it is worth considering favourably horses from yards proven to be in form, and being circumspect about backing those from yards that, currently, are not.

Possible reasons for longer-than-normal but not over-protracted absence from the course can range from recovery from a relatively minor setback to a ground-dependent horse waiting for suitable going – for example, a soft-ground specialist waiting out a period of dry weather, or vice versa. If there is evidence that this may be the case (perhaps the horse you are interested in has run all his best races on soft ground, but it's been baking hot for the last two months), the time-span without a run should not be seen as a deterrent.

Trainer/Yard Form

Another of the many indications that horses are living beings, not ciphers, is that even the very best and most successful trainers will experience times when virtually every horse in the yard is running out of his skin, and other times when they start to wonder when they'll ever train another winner. Furthermore, these circumstances can shift from one end of the spectrum to the other in a remarkably short space of time. Obviously, if a yard hits the doldrums, a trainer will do everything in his power to discover the reason, but sometimes this may be elusive. Since racehorses are highly trained athletes, competing against others of the same kind, it is easy to see that a performance drop off of just a couple of percentage points can make the difference between winning and not performing very well. One common cause of loss of performance is a low-grade virus in the yard. While more serious diseases may exhibit obvious symptoms, minor ones can sneak under the radar – even the regular blood testing carried out by many trainers may show up little or nothing until a horse who has run below expectations shows some abnormality when tested post-race. With an increasing understanding of such scenarios, it is becoming more common for trainers who have concerns to 'shut down' their yards for a while (and thus have no runners) until there is evidence at home that the horses are recovering from whatever ails them. This often proves remarkably effective, in that the horses, given time to recover fully, return to the track in such good heart that the yard starts turning out winner after winner.

What about a horse whose last race was very recent? There may be different reasons for this. Some trainers are known to run their horses quite regularly while they're fit and well (perhaps weekly, for several weeks in succession), and this should not be seen as a negative. (Occasionally, a horse may even run, and win, on successive days, but this tends to happen in lower-grade, less competitive races and a horse who won within the previous twenty-four hours may not be the best proposition in a more competitive affair.) Another reason why a horse may make a pretty quick reappearance after a success is to have another race before his official rating is increased by the handicapper (handicappers don't make instantaneous changes to horses' ratings, but do so periodically) or, in a conditions race, to similarly avoid a date-related penalty.

12. **Additional equipment.** Sometimes, horses are fitted with additional equipment besides the saddle and bridle. The intentions behind this are varied, and this equipment is discussed further in the section, In the Paddock in Chapter 7. However, some of this equipment is intended to have a positive effect on a horse's performance and must be declared in advance of the race, and thus will usually be indicated on a racecard. The most common of these are blinkers (**B** – if it's the first time these have been applied for a race, this may be indicated as **B1**), visor **(V)**, hood **(H)**, cheekpieces (**P** for pieces, to avoid confusion with **C** for course winner) and tongue tie **(T)**.* Assessing the potential influence of these devices is difficult without knowing whether they have been used previously and, if so, whether or not the influence seemed positive. Even from the trainer's viewpoint, there may be an element of experiment in adding such equipment. Perhaps the most significant items to note, if it is apparent that they are being applied for the first time, are blinkers and tongue ties. Blinkers will sometimes 'sharpen up' a horse, causing him to travel more enthusiastically and, if this happens within reason, they may produce significant improvement. In other cases, however, they can cause a horse to run much too freely and thus have a detrimental effect. The application of a tongue tie may suggest that there has been some concern about a horse's breathing during the race, in which malpositioning of his tongue can play a part. If that diagnosis is correct, a device that helps keep the tongue in position can, again, bring about improvement, but this cannot be guaranteed in advance of the race in which it is first fitted. However, if the horse's previous form indicates that he has run respectable races with a tongue tie fitted, it is reasonable to assume that it works for him.

---

*Following a BHA decision in autumn 2017, it is now a requirement for a trainer to declare that a horse has had a breathing operation since his previous run, and some cards may now indicate this by **WS** (presumably for wind surgery). Infectious diseases aside, horses can suffer from several conditions that may compromise the mechanical efficiency of their breathing to a greater or lesser extent, and even a relatively small reduction in air intake will hamper a horse trying to gallop flat out. There are now some quite minor procedures that can be of significant benefit in some cases and there have been examples of horses showing significant improvement after one of these, hence the decision that all such should be in the public domain. However, as with many surgical procedures the benefits, if any, have to be judged on a case-by-case basis and it is not inevitably the case that a horse will improve following treatment.

13. **Reference to horse's previous success in a race with some similarity to today's.** The various symbols discussed below are sometimes grouped together. In the example, **CD** means that the horse is a course and distance winner. A horse who has been racing successfully for some time might have the symbols **C2, CD3, D2** against his name, indicating that he has twice won at the course over a distance different from today's race, he has won three times over today's course and distance, and he has twice won over today's distance at a different course. These indicators are clearly useful, but may still need to be viewed with a little discretion.

   To take **CD** first, the fact that a horse has previously won at today's course and distance has to be seen as a positive, but in terms of his chances in today's race, it still needs to be viewed in context with his weight (*see* point 17) and current ground conditions (*see* point 15).

   C alone means that the horse has previously won at the course, but over a different distance. This *can* be a positive, particularly on a course with distinctive characteristics, such as being undulating, prone to extreme ground conditions, sharply left- or right-handed, etc. However, it can also be inconsequential, or even potentially misleading, depending on circumstances. In flat racing, for instance, many courses have a straight of sufficient length that sprint races (and sometimes races of a mile or so) can be run on the straight track, whereas longer races will involve turns, which may be quite sharp. For example, Haydock Park runs races of 5 and 6 furlongs on the straight, but longer races are run on a fairly sharp left-handed course. Although it is *entirely possible* that he will do so, there is *no guarantee* that a horse who has won there over, say, 6 furlongs as a two-year-old will be suited by longer races on the **round course** at a later stage – he may, for example, turn out to be a horse who is better suited by a right-handed track.

   The opposite of a course winner is, clearly, one who has not won at the particular course before. If further study of form suggests that he has run there several times, apparently quite poorly, this may mean that he is unsuited to the course characteristics, which would clearly be a negative. Of course, if it turns out that he has never raced at this course before, it is harder to form an opinion. However, if he has previously done well (or badly) at a course with similar characteristics, this may offer a clue. To give an example from the flat, the old turf course at Lingfield has a significant downhill run towards the straight, followed by a left-hand turn into it. These features are similar to those of Epsom, so it is not unreasonable to think that a horse who has handled the former is likely to handle the latter. Conversely, an apparent inability to cope with one may be replicated at the other.

   A **D** against a horse indicates that he has previously won over the distance of the current race. This, usually, can be considered a positive – it shows that he has the speed or stamina, or blend of the two, to seem suited by it. However, there may be some caveats to consider. To take one example from the flat, Epsom and Sandown (along with most other courses) both have sprint races over 5 furlongs. However, a horse might have won three or four such races at one of these courses, but never have performed (or might prove not to perform) so effectively at the other. This is because the 5 furlong course at Epsom is mainly downhill (quite significantly, at points), whereas the one at Sandown is significantly uphill. Thus the horse who does well at Epsom might run out of steam in the closing stages at Sandown, while one who does well at Sandown may be 'taken off his feet' at Epsom and not have the sheer speed to be competitive. This sort of scenario will not always apply – some horses are pretty versatile and may prove successful on tracks with quite different characteristics. However, *assuming* that this will be so, without pretty firm evidence, can be quite risky.

14. **BF** means beaten favourite – the horse started favourite on his previous outing, but didn't win (finished 2nd, in this example). It is easy to see this as a negative and, in some cases, further investigation may bear this out – for example, if the horse started a red-hot favourite last time out and ran very disappointingly. However, if he started 7–1 favourite in a competitive field of twenty runners, and was narrowly beaten into third place, he may actually have run right up to his best form, only for **'the market'** to get things slightly wrong.

   If a horse has been beaten favourite in perhaps his two or three previous runs, this will be shown as **BF2** or **BF3**. Particularly in the latter case, it then becomes legitimate to start wondering whether (a) his connections have an inflated view of his ability, and are lumping the family silver on a 'swan' who is really a 'goose' or (b) whether the horse really does have an attitude problem in respect of putting his best hoof forward. However, it should be borne in mind that horses do not win races because they are made favourite – they are made favourite because the market hopes they will win, which is not the same thing.

15. **Ground conditions.** Some newspapers follow the course and distance symbols with others that effect to show the horse's preference for particular going, normally using abbreviations such as **F** (firm), **GF** (good to firm), **G** (good), **GS** (good to soft), **S** (soft) and **HY** (heavy). (Other definitions of going sometimes seen used are 'standard', which is the term used for all-weather tracks under most circumstances, and 'yielding', a term used particularly in Irish racing that pretty much approximates to 'good to soft'.)

   In principle, this should be quite helpful and can be so if it matches previous successes on going to that which is actually in force for the current race (e.g. **GS** if that is the actual prevailing going). However, since they can't predict actual weather conditions, these papers tend to mention successes on ground similar to the conditions they *think* likely to pertain to the current race. Thus, if the forecast going is good, they may mention only previous victories on that ground, whereas a more in-depth analysis of form may show that a horse is more versatile in respect of ground conditions than these symbols suggest.

   That said, it is very useful to know whether an individual horse has a preference for a particular type of going and/or an aversion to another type. Although some

All-weather Irony

There is a certain irony here regarding turf and all-weather surfaces. When the latter were pioneered for various equestrian activities, the original intention was to produce an artificial surface that mimicked, as closely as possible, the surface offered by natural downland turf. While artificial surfaces have proved of great benefit to horse sports, it is a fact that some racehorses perform better on either turf or all-weather tracks.

horses are very versatile in this respect, others, for sound physiological reasons, are very ground-dependent (*see* the entries for action and conformation in Chapter 8 for a further discussion of this).

16. **Name of trainer** (*on course racecards, location of training establishment may be added*). This can be useful information, because it may indicate a trainer known to be in good form (*see also* point 11) and, if the location of his yard is included, it will give a clue to how far the horses has travelled to the race – not always significant, but it can be on the basis of the question: 'Why pay to send a horse to the other end of the country if you don't think he's got much chance?' On the other hand, of course, in times of bad weather, that may be the only course fit for racing.

17. **Horse's age and today's weight carried, in that order.** The actual weight carried is usually relevant mainly in comparison with what the other horses are carrying – for instance, 9st 7lb is a high weight in a flat handicap, when the horse in question may be conceding a stone and a half to others at the foot of the handicap, but in a level weights race, all horses will be carrying it. The time when the actual weight itself may be more significant is in long-distance races on soft ground, when a high weight may be effectively an extra burden and a low weight an extra advantage.

18. **Name of jockey, and allowance, if any.** The topic of jockey categories and allowances (or 'claims') was discussed in Chapter 3. Some races are open only to apprentices/conditional jockeys and/or amateurs. However, trainers will often use such riders in valuable races in which most jockeys are fully-fledged professionals. (As mentioned in Chapter 2, in some high-class races, riders who would normally claim an allowance are not permitted to do so, but are allowed to ride. Although, for obvious reasons, this happens infrequently, it does occasionally, usually if the rider has previously struck up a successful relationship with the horse and clearly gets on with him. Nevertheless, this is quite an accolade for an up-and-coming jockey.)

    The usual reason why a trainer will use an apprentice or conditional jockey is the fairly obvious one of taking a few pounds off a horse's back in a competitive race. In fairly crude terms, this can be seen as a 'punt' that the weight allowance will more than counteract the jockey's relative inexperience. Inevitably, a jockey who has had perhaps only twenty race-rides will be, by definition, less experienced than a seasoned professional and, on that basis, perhaps more likely to make a tactical error, or be a little less technically proficient. In practice, however, it can be a shrewd move that often proves decisive. With the current accent on educating young jockeys, it is now the case that virtually all young apprentices/conditionals are very proficient riders, and there is regular evidence that many prove 'good value for their allowance'. Therefore, if a successful trainer 'puts up' a young rider in a big race, this needn't be seen as a discouraging move.

    The situation with amateurs can be a little different because some keen amateurs will have their own horses, and will be keen to ride them whenever circumstances allow. This doesn't make them bad riders – some are very far from it – but it doesn't necessarily make them what would be (given the option) the trainer's first choice. Amateur races are probably best watched with interest until an opinion can be formed of various riders' skills – a remark that applies also to point-to-points. (In case these remarks seem disparaging, I should make the point that amateur riders have been successful in races as big as the Grand National – three times, in fact, since 1980 – and that all require a rider's licence, which is only available to those who have proved, in normal riding terms, to be pretty capable.

19. **Rating.** *On course racecards, the number here is likely to be the BHA official rating for the horse – i.e. the rating that will dictate his handicap mark, and/or which races he is qualified to enter. In other journals it may be a figure based on their racing correspondent's or other staff member's private assessment. These 'unofficial' numbers take various forms. Some are, in effect 'private handicaps', in which the individual is doing something broadly similar to the official handicapper, but using his own judgement; others are based on trying to analyse relative times of races and individual horses. Although sometimes the horse 'top-rated' by such systems will win, my advice is to take them with a pinch of salt.*

20. **Colour, sex and parentage of the horse.** These details will usually appear on course racecards; they are also available in the form section of dedicated racing journals.

    The following abbreviations are commonly used for colour:
    b = bay. The most common colour for a Thoroughbred; a main coat that is a shade of brown, with black mane, tail and lower legs.
    br = brown. Normally a mid-brown without the black extremities that would define bay.
    ch = chestnut.* A more or less ginger coat colour: some horses with this colouration have a lighter (flaxen) mane and tail.
    bl = black. Very few horses are truly black, being more often very dark brown, however, they are described as black when they appear nearly so.
    gr = grey. This may be seen in various shades, from very dark ('iron grey') to much lighter. Indeed, most grey horses become much lighter as they age, until they are visually white. Nonetheless, they are still known, throughout the equestrian world, as 'grey'. Truly white horses are extremely rare and are pretty much genetic freaks.
    ro = roan. Fairly rare in Thoroughbreds, a roan coat is a fairly even mixture of 'white' hairs with another colour, seen over most of the body, although the mane and tail are often 'solid' areas of the 'other' colour.
       A horse's colour has no impact on his racing ability, but it can be useful in terms of picking him out in a packed field, provided that it is one of the less common ones. Similarly, markings such as a blaze (white facial marking) or white legs can be useful.

    The following abbreviations are commonly used for sex:
    h = horse. Actually used to mean a mature entire (not gelded) horse – one who is physically a stallion. In racing the term is usually applied to an animal aged five years or older.
    c = colt. In racing, an entire male aged four or younger (the very young are called colt foals).

---

*There used to be a convention that, when used to describe a Thoroughbred, this was spelt 'chesnut'.

Grey horses always catch the eye, and are usually easy to spot in a race – this horse looks white, but grey will still be his official colour.

g = gelding. A castrated male – most males not intended for breeding are gelded, as are some individuals who are very difficult temperamentally.
m = mare. In racing, a female aged five or more.
f = filly. In racing, a female aged four or younger; the female equivalent of a colt. (Females are not neutered.)

As explained in Chapter 2, where males and females meet in races other than handicaps, the latter will receive a weight allowance from the former. Also, depending on the conditions of the race, there may be a weight allowance given to younger entries by their older rivals. The idea behind this is that the allowance should balance out any difference in strength, maturity, etc. between the contestants inherent in sex and/or age difference.

Parentage can be a significant factor in helping to determine the sort of distance at which a horse is likely to be most effective and, possibly, preference for ground conditions. This is not surprising since speed, stamina and physical confirmation, which can be major influences on these criteria, are likely to be passed on genetically. However, these are not rules set in stone, and actual past performances by an individual will either support, or tend to negate, assumptions made on the basis of breeding.

21. **Owner and breeder details** *are likely to appear on course racecards;* they are also available in the form section of dedicated racing journals. These details are likely to be of little significance to most race-goers, unless the owner is, perhaps, a famous actor or sportsperson (there are quite a few).

22. **Illustration/description of colours worn by the jockey.** *Any written description is likely to accompany an actual illustration on a course racecard.* Racing journals and (sometimes) regular newspapers will show the illustration only, just for major races. Noting the colours is pretty much essential if you want to follow your fancy. NB the colours are not chosen by the jockey, but are those registered to the horse's owner(s) and will be worn on all that owner's horses. If an owner runs more than one horse in the race, there will be minor changes for identification, usually in the form of a different colour/pattern of cap.

23. **Racecard number/order** is determined as follows. In handicaps, it will be determined by each horse's weight – highest weight will be number one; lowest weight will be the highest number. If more than one horse is allotted the same weight, the horse whose name is first alphabetically will come above the others with that same weight. In level weights races, horses will be numbered by their relative position in the alphabet, starting from A. In conditions races, horses will be numbered alphabetically by their weight allocation, so all those with 9st 7lb will be numbered alphabetically, then all those with, say 9st 3lb alphabetically, then all those with, say 8st 12lb. For example:

    1. Stopped Dead   9st 7lb
    2. Where Am I   9st 7lb
    3. Fast Asleep   9st 3lb
    4. Full Of Hay   9st 3lb
    5. Dashing Home   8st 12lb
    6. Energy To Burn   8st 12lb

24. **The betting forecast is simply what some reasonably well-informed person involved in compiling the card thinks the runners' odds are likely to be.** Although, on the whole, it will probably indicate which horses are likely to be well fancied, and which are not, it is basically guesswork made some time before the race and cannot be relied upon in terms of significant accuracy.

25. **Pundit's view.** As with 24, this will be a potted comment by someone regarding their view of certain horses' prospects and the possible outcome of the race. Bearing in mind that most racing journalists tip more losers than winners, this should not be taken as gospel. That said, in dedicated racing journals and on racecards, the writer is likely to be pretty well informed – for instance, some official racecards base their comments on a well-regarded publication called *Timeform*.

26. **Records of favourites** in the last few years are, to my mind, usually of no significance (although the fact that a particular horse has won the race previously, and is running again, may be worthy of consideration – *see* point 28).

27. **Ages of previous winners** can be significant, particularly where conditions races are concerned, because a particular trend might suggest that a certain age bracket is favoured by the conditions. For example, if a conditions flat race open to three-year-olds and upward is won regularly by a three-year-old, this may suggest that these horses have an advantage over their older rivals under the prevailing weight allowance. If, however, three-year-olds have been generally unsuccessful, this may suggest that the weight allowance is usually insufficient for them. Age allowances (which are an old concept, first visited by Admiral Rous in the mid-nineteenth century) and sex allowances (a more recent construct) have always been subject to debate and are likely to remain so.

28. **Previous winners.** As noted under point 26, if a horse is entered in a race he won the previous year, this past performance means that his renewed presence is note-worthy – he is, at least, a course and distance winner. However, in trying to assess his chance this time round, it is important to look at details such as his recent form, whether the prevailing going is similar this year to last (if not, is he ground-dependent?) and, if the race is a handicap, whether his current rating is significantly higher than last year.

In summary, if you are really interested in trying to find winners (or, at least, horses likely to give you a run for your money), it is worth familiarizing yourself with the information provided on racecards and the form sections of racing journals, and learning to evaluate what bare figures and symbols may signify. However, my own view is that learning more about individual horses, forming your own opinion about their strengths and weaknesses, is a great way to get more involved in the sport – and backing a winner on the basis of your own deliberations is always more satisfying than backing one because the pundit in your newspaper tipped him.

CHAPTER 6

Betting

There is no requirement or necessity for anyone at a race meeting to have a bet, and many enthusiasts for the sport can happily watch a whole afternoon's racing simply enjoying the sport and perhaps noting the performance of certain horses for another occasion. Other race-goers may simply have one or two bets on horses they really fancy, whilst keeping their money in their pockets while the other races unfold.

That said, having a modest financial interest in a race does add a certain spice for many people, and there is no harm in betting in modest amounts 'for fun' – provided that this is the true intention. Some people do, in fact, go racing with an amount of money set aside as their 'bank', considering this to be part of the day's expenditure, and feeling happy if they actually get it back, or make enough profit to buy a round of drinks. Although this is understandable if it is truly affordable, it would still make more sense to avoid betting on races that seem truly impenetrable on the basis that doing so is likely to mean lower losses/more funds available to back horses you actually fancy.

While I make no claims that reading this chapter will ensure that you bet profitably, I do hope that it will:

- Offer a basic explanation of how bookmaking works – which is the driving force behind why the odds on horses will vary.
- Explain what the numbers mean in terms of fractional odds.
- Explain the difference between bookmakers and pool betting.
- Explain how to place bets.
- Highlight the concept of betting rationally – this doesn't necessarily mean 'successfully', but it does mean applying an element of logic to your bets.

Don't Believe the Old Movies

In case you have any concerns about dealing with bookmakers that are rooted in old black and white movies featuring razor gangs and shifty syringe-wielding characters breaking into stable yards, you should be reassured. Bookmaking businesses in the UK must be licensed by the Gambling Commission, and those who operate at racecourses do so under the supervision of the AGT (Administration Of Gambling On Tracks Ltd). In the unlikely event of any dispute with a racecourse bookie, you can ask for assistance from the course betting ring manager. In all the years I have been backing horses, I've never had any issue with being paid out on a successful bet.

A line of bookmakers, ready to do business.

THE PRINCIPLES OF BOOKMAKING

If you are going to bet on horses it is useful to have a basic understanding of how bookmaking works. The underlying principle for bookmakers is to take bets in a way that shades the odds in their favour so that, whichever horse wins, they have taken more money overall on the race than they are obliged to pay out in winnings. (Having used the term 'shade' I should add that there is nothing 'shady' about this – it is simply astute arithmetic.)

By way of illustration, imagine a scenario in which there are six horses in a race, but no one – neither the connections nor the bookies – knows anything about their relative merits. With nothing else to go on, the mathematical odds against each horse would be 5–1 (quite literally, five against one). Now suppose that the bookie priced up all the runners at these odds and (because there was no form guidance for the punters) an equal amount of money in total (say £1,000) was placed on each horse – we would then have a situation where the bookie had taken £6,000 in bets. However, whichever horse won, at odds of 5–1, he would have to pay out this amount on winning bets, in the form of the £5,000 actual winnings and £1,000 in returning the **stakes** (the money handed over by punters to establish the bets). Thus, the bookie has made neither a loss nor a profit.

Now imagine the same scenario of six unknown horses, in which the bookie priced each of them up not at 5–1, but at 4–1. Again, let's say £1,000 is placed on each horse in

Understanding Odds

Odds are the number of units a bookie will pay out to a single unit of a winning bet, for example 3–1 will pay £3 to a £1 bet (plus the £1 'stake' is returned). Sometimes when, for reasons explained below, bookies want to adjust the odds on particular horses, they will fine-tune them by using fractional odds (a little like giving something a mark of 7½ out of 10). It is in these cases that you may see odds such as 5–2, 15–8, etc. These can seem complicated but can be rationalized by dividing the first figure by the second so that, in these examples, 5–2 becomes 2½–1 and 15–8 becomes $1^7/_8$–1. By way of further example, you will see that 15–8 represents slightly shorter odds than 2–1 (which would be 16–8).

Fractional odds do not require that you bet in the units quoted. For example, if a horse is 15–8, you do not have to place a bet of £8, because these odds are $1^7/_8$–1 *to any stake at all*, so, for example a £10 bet at £15–8 will pay £18.75 (plus your stake back).

bets: the bookie has, again, taken a total of £6,000, but what happens now when the result is announced? This time, because the odds of the winner are 4–1, the bookie has to pay out £4,000 in actual winnings, and return £1,000 in winning stakes (a total of £5,000) and has thus made a profit of £1,000.

Real-life scenarios are, of course, vastly more complex than this (it's impossible to visualize circumstances in which no one knew anything about – or at least had an opinion about – six horses), but this is the template on which bookmaking is based. The aim for a bookmaker is to produce an opening book in which the odds against each horse are, mathematically at least, in his favour. One way of looking at this is to say that (beyond something truly bizarre happening) there is a 100 per cent chance that the race will be won by one of the horses in it. The chances of each horse, depending on his perceived merits, can thus be represented by a proportion of 100 per cent. Suppose a bookie thinks that a particular horse has a 10 per cent chance of winning (and thus a 90 per cent chance that he won't), that equates to odds of 9–1. However, to shade the odds in his favour, the bookie may actually price the horse up at 8–1 (which, in percentage terms, equates to 12½ per cent: 8 x 12½ = 100). If the same principle is applied to all the horses in a race, when all the shortened odds are converted to percentages and added up, the total will come to more than 100 per cent. This, known in the trade as 'an over-round book', is the starting point for taking bets on each race.

Of course, this starting point is based on the bookie's own opinion and his task is then to adjust the odds in response to the amount of money actually bet on each horse, to try to ensure that he has taken more money in bets overall than he will be liable to pay out, whichever horse wins the race. (In practice, not all bookies manage to do this on all races, but it is their business model and they need to achieve it in most cases if they are to have a viable business.)

The factors that influence the actual betting on any particular race are many and varied. At one end of the spectrum are 'coincidence' plunges by punters (loads of people backing a horse called Boxing Day running on Boxing Day, or similar); at the other end there are scenarios such as a sudden change in the weather producing extreme going that is likely to favour one horse distinctly more than another. In between are factors such as a favoured jockey having a purple patch, evidence from another meeting that a stable that has been in the doldrums has suddenly returned to form, and many others, one of which is a 'snowball effect' whereby punters see that the odds on a particular horse have begun to shorten, assume that 'someone knows something', and back it themselves, adding to what becomes a 'plunge' on that horse.

Whatever reason people have for backing various horses, that is all 'weight of money' the bookie has to consider, and his response will be a mixture of personal judgement and hard-headed accounting. The proportions of these qualities will depend, in part, on the bookie's confidence in his own judgement, and his attitude to risk. In times past, it was not unusual for bookies to rely heavily on their own judgement – sometimes with spectacular results in terms of either fortune or ruin – but nowadays the majority are less risk-adverse. However, on occasion, some still choose to 'stand' a horse to a certain extent – this means, in effect, that they will accrue more liabilities on a horse than accountancy/discretion might dictate, because they think less of this horse's chances than the punters backing him. In this respect they are, in effect, veering towards becoming punters themselves. Generally, however, a bookie will seek to balance the books (in his favour) by following more closely the 'accountancy' route. This involves changing the odds in response to money placed (or not) on the whole field by shortening or lengthening them. Although a bookie will, to an extent, take notice of the odds offered by other bookies, his main concern will be the bets he takes himself. For example, if a punter places a large bet on a horse at the current odds, the bookie, having taken the bet, is likely to shorten the odds, because his liabilities if that horse wins have increased, and he actually doesn't want any more money on that horse at present. The fact that he is now quoting 4–1, when the bookies either side of him are showing 5–1 doesn't bother him – it's actually what he wants for the time being.

In addition to shortening the odds on the heavily backed horse, the bookie may try to rebalance his book by lengthening the odds on horses he really doesn't think can win. The purpose behind this is to entice punters into backing them, so he has more money in his satchel to pay out on the big bet. Since, in most races, there will be some horses with little discernible chance, and there will usually be someone willing to have small bets on them on a 'stick a pin in basis', or because an **outsider** has the same name as their cat, this can help the bookie's cause. There is the potential downside that there might be a shock result but, even if the bookie has to pay out on small bets placed at long odds, this may still save his bacon if the result means that he doesn't have to pay out on the big bet that lost.

One technique that smaller bookies may use to avoid a potential problem if they have overstretched themselves in respect to their liabilities on a particular horse is called 'laying-off'. This is a safety measure for the bookie that doesn't affect the punter(s) who have backed the horse in question. Suppose, for example, the bookie had taken £2,000 in bets on a horse at 4–1, and really thinks that this horse is likely to win, in which case he'd have to pay back the £2,000 bet plus £8,000 in winnings. If he can pass on these liabilities to another, bigger, concern, he has the opportunity to avoid a considerable risk. If he can place his own £2,000 bet at 4–1 (or thereabouts) then, if the horse wins, he can pay his punters with his own winnings; if the horse loses, his own bet loses, but he is reimbursed by the losing bets placed by his punters. Alternatively, he can place a smaller bet than needed to cover his liabilities on this horse, which introduces a modest risk/reward scenario. If, for example, his own bet is just £1,500 at 4–1, if the horse wins then he has won just £6,000; he still has to pay £8,000 in winnings, but has reduced his losses. However, if the horse loses, he has lost his £1,500, but has taken £2,000 in losing bets, so is up £500.

Principles of Betting with Bookmakers

As mentioned, real-life bookmaking is more complex than the broad principles explained above, and real-life betting has the potential to become so, too. However, I hope that newcomers to racing will be content to place simple bets in modest amounts primarily for fun, and my emphasis here will be on describing the basics of placing simple cash bets with on-course or High Street bookmakers.

In practice, although a novice race-goer might place a bet or two with their local bookie on the way to the races, it is more likely that any bets will be placed on the course. However, there are some points to learn from how High Street bookies function that may be helpful in a racecourse scenario, so we'll look at the former first.

If you go to place a bet in a local betting shop on race day, you will usually have the option of either 'taking a price' or placing the bet at 'starting price' (*see* below).

Taking a price means placing a bet at the odds currently on offer. In a betting shop, the current odds for a race will usually be shown on one of the screens. So, if you fancy Waddleslikeaduck in the 2.40 at Beverley, and the current odds are 20–1, you write out your bet on a betting slip and tell the person at the counter that you will 'take the twenties'. They will then write that price on your betting slip (which you will put in a safe place for later). In due course, Waddleslikeaduck may either drift in the market, or be the subject of a late gamble, and his starting price may be, for example, 25–1 or 16–1 but if he waddles past the post first, you will traditionally and usually be paid out at the price you took earlier. (This is not always the cases nowadays, because some bookmaking firms may offer 'a best odds' system whereby they will pay out at starting price if these odds are better than those you took earlier. However, this cannot be assumed without checking.)

The alternative is to place your bet at the starting price (which you won't know at the time), but which will happen automatically if you just write '2.40 Beverley Waddleslikeaduck £5 win [or whatever]' on your betting slip. The best reason for doing this is if you think that the horse's odds may lengthen during the day, so that he may start at bigger odds than those on show – although this will be a matter for conjecture. (The other reason is if the bookies' screens are showing CGI imaginary racing from a non-existent venue, and you just think 'life's too short …')

So, what is this mysterious 'starting price'? In simple terms, starting prices (SPs) are prices returned by officials from the racecourse as an approximate average of the prices on offer from course bookies immediately before a race started. If, for example, half of them were offering 7–1 and half were offering 8–1 on a particular horse, it is likely that the SP would be **returned at** 15–2 (7½–1).

Normally, when betting on-course, the SP won't be available unless one of the major bookmakers has a shop within the course buildings and you bet accordingly. Instead, you will 'take the price' available at the time you make the bet. One thing that adds spice to placing bets on-course is to wander up and down the line of bookies trying to find the best price to take. Even if your bet is a small one, it is satisfying finding a bookie who will lay you, say, 16–1 when his colleagues are offering 14–1. Variations like this do exist, so it's worth checking. Generally, racecourse bookies will start to price up the runners in the next race about ten to fifteen minutes after the preceding one has been run. At that time, the overall market will just be forming and the odds for the individual runners may be quite volatile. If, at this stage, there are odds available on a horse you fancy, it may be worth taking the current price, on the assumption that (a) you are

Writing Bets in a High Street Shop

In a betting shop, if you are placing several bets, you don't have to write each individual bet on a separate sheet. You could, for example, do as follows:

1.30 Sandown Roadhump £2 each way*

2.05 Carlisle Turned To Stone £4 win

3.30 Warwick Petrified £3 each way*

Total £14

*See Each Way and Place Betting, later.
The constraints are not to cram too much on one slip, and to keep things fairly legible.

happy with it and (b) that, in your view, the odds are more likely to shorten than to lengthen (time may, of course, prove you wrong, but that's part of the game). If, on the other hand, the odds everywhere are shorter than seems attractive (*see* Value later in this chapter), you may choose to wait in the hope that they will lengthen as other horses are backed.

If, having compared the odds between bookies, you decide to place a bet, the way to do it is to say: 'Five pounds [or whatever] Waddleslikeaduck' and mention the price you are taking. The bookie will repeat this, and give you a printed betting slip confirming the bet, whilst ramming your fiver into the dark recesses of his satchel.

POOL BETTING

In many countries other than the UK, betting doesn't take place with bookmakers, but with various 'pool' systems. Within the UK, a similar system has existed for years, known as the Tote. Set up as a statutory corporation in 1928, it was sold into private hands in 2011 with a seven-year licence to continue offering pool bets. For many years, Tote outlets have been a standard alternative to regular bookmakers at racecourses, and it has been possible to bet with the organization via High Street premises, (formerly) by phone and (latterly) the internet. At the time of writing, with the Tote licence agreement about to expire, it seems that the majority of UK racecourses will set up an alternative pool operation that will offer a variety of betting options broadly common to most pool systems. To avoid any possible confusion arising from specific names, this section will refer simply to 'pool betting'.

Whereas bookmakers set initial odds on a race and adjust them as they deem necessary, pool betting operates differently. Punters bet on their fancy in set units of money (buying the number of units they wish to), all of which goes into a pool. From this, the pool operator takes a percentage; the remainder is available to be divided up proportionately between winning tickets. Suppose, for example, the pool (after the operator's cut) was £20,000, if there were 1,000 winning units, each unit would be paid £20; if there were 2,000, each would be paid £10, and so on. A punter who had bought more than one unit would get the pro rata payout – in the examples given, someone with five units out of the 1,000 would get £100; with five units out of 2,000, £50.

You will see from this example that, in pool betting, the amount paid out on a winning bet derives simply from the total amount bet on the event divided by the number of winning units. Theoretically, it is possible for a winning horse who is a hot favourite with traditional bookmakers to pay really well on a pool system, if few people back him on the latter, or for a winner who is an outsider with the bookmakers to pay poorly on a pool system if lots of people back him that way. In practice, because many people prefer to bet with one or other system, there is usually a broad similarity between book- ies' odds and those of a pool, but differences can still be significant. To provide some comparison between current bookies' odds and pool dividends, while money is being taken in the lead-up to a race, pool screens may offer running approximations of what the payout would be *at that given moment* on the different runners. For example, a horse might be 7–1 with most bookies, but showing at 9.2 (pool systems use decimals, not fractions) on a pool system which, *at that time*, would make the latter more attrac- tive, although subject to change. (Thus, with a pool system, you don't 'take the price' as with a bookie, but basically 'take a chance' on what the final dividend might be.) Another point to note is that while, with a bookie, you get your stake back on a winning bet, with pool systems, the amount quoted is the *total return* per unit.

When pool betting, rather than giving the horse's name, you give his racecard number, so you need to be careful to give the correct number rather than, for instance, his draw number. Also, when placing a single bet, ensure that you cite the correct race time.

EACH WAY AND PLACE BETTING

The explanations about betting so far have been mainly concerned with the basic prin- ciples so, for ease of explanation, I've talked in terms of win bets on single horses. In practice, it is also possible to back horses to be placed, which we'll look at here, and to have multiple bets, which we'll look at in basic terms later in this chapter.

Each Way Bets

These bets are placed with bookies, either on the High Street or on the course. Where practical, it is easier to place them with the former, since betting shops handle them all the time as part of their normal service whereas, traditionally, a lot of on-course bookies didn't like them, and many didn't take them, presumably because they compli- cate making a 'book' and because fiddling around to find the change needed to pay out small returns on placed horses could be an irritation to a busy bookie. Nowadays, perhaps aided by computerized systems, more on-course bookies do take each way bets, and this will usually be advertised on their pitch, but it is worth checking their place payout terms.

An each way bet is actually two bets written/expressed as a single bet that covers not only the prospect of the horse winning, but also of him not winning but being placed. Precisely what this term means will vary according to the number of runners, the type of race and the individual bookie's terms of trading, and some typical examples are given below. Prior to discussing this, the key points to note are that the 'placed' element of the bet will be at much reduced odds (no bookie is going to offer the same odds for a horse to finish first, second or third as for him just to win – that would be financial suicide) and that the cost of an each way bet includes the value of both the win and place element. For example, a £5 each way bet means £5 on the horse to win, and £5 on him to be placed, therefore it costs £10'. Why, then', you might ask, 'should I not have the whole £10 to win, and thus get paid out at the full odds?' That's a fair question at first sight, but it presupposes that the horse *will* win. (The obvious response to the question is that, if you're so sure the horse will win, why not put more money on him anyway – but that might not be responsible of me, so pretend you haven't read it.)

The reasons for considering an each way bet can be illustrated as follows. First, in a competitive race (let's say with nine runners) suppose that the horse you fancy is one of perhaps three you can see being involved in the finish. Because these horses, and perhaps a couple of others, will have their supporters, the odds against the fancied horses, including yours, are quite favourable. Let's say yours is 9–2 (4½–1). Now, while you think he *could* win, you know there's not much between him and a couple of the other runners, so it's entirely possible that he could run well and just be beaten.

'Placed' and Place Odds

The term 'placed' is sometimes used casually to refer to horses who have finished in the first three, but when betting it is safest to view it in the context of what it means from a betting perspective – i.e. whether it signifies that certain bets will be successful (or not). The winner of a race is always considered to be 'placed' (i.e. first) and therefore, if you back a horse for a place on a pool system (*see* Place Betting) and he wins, you have a successful bet. Other than that, whether a horse is placed for *betting purposes* depends on the number of runners and, to some extent, the type of race. In recent times, there has been some consolidation of terms among bookmakers and the following are fairly standard nowadays:

Race of four or fewer runners – no place betting – win only.
Five to seven runners – bookies pay place terms on first two (typically a quarter the odds for the place).
Eight or more runners – bookies pay place terms on first three (typically one-fifth the odds for a place).
In handicaps only:
Twelve to fifteen runners – bookies pay place terms on first three (typically a quarter the odds for a place).
Sixteen to twenty-one runners – bookies pay place terms on first four (typically one-fifth the odds for a place).
Twenty-two or more runners – bookies pay place terms on first four (typically a quarter the odds for a place.
It is still worth checking the place terms on offer from a course bookie if you intend to bet each way. Also, if you are betting in a High Street shop, it is worth noting whether they are offering 'special' each way odds on big races with a lot of runners (e.g. perhaps paying on the fifth horse).

However, you are reasonably confident that he can finish in the first three. If he comes second or third, and you back him each way, although the 'win' part of your bet will lose, the 'place' part will virtually recover your losses, so you've had an almost 'free' win bet. Assuming that the place terms for this race are one-fifth of the 'win' odds – which would be usual for a nine-runner race – this example works as follows. Let's say you have a £5 each way bet, costing £10. Your £5 win bet loses, but your £5 place bet is successful, paying £4.50 plus your £5 place stake back, so the bookie gives you £9.50 and you've lost just 50p on the race. (Of course, if your horse does win, you get that £9.50 plus the win element of the bet, an additional return of £27.50.)

The second occasion when an each way bet may be prudent is in competitive, big-field handicaps where, because of the nature of the race, most of the runners are at relatively long odds. In such races, it is entirely reasonable that a horse with a decent chance of finishing **in the frame** could be at odds of, let's say, 16–1. Because of the very nature of such races, it is usually difficult for anyone to be sure which horse will win, so betting on them is necessarily speculative – more about making a case for a horse who can reasonably be expected to be 'thereabouts' at the finish. Backing horses just to win in such races is, to my mind, unnecessarily risky when, with sixteen runners or more, each way/place bets in handicaps will pay on the first four. At the example odds of 16–1, a finisher in the first four will earn you either 4–1 the place (at a quarter the odds a place) or just over 3–1 (at a fifth of the odds a place) – and remember, if he does win, you get the 16–1 win as well.

Another reason for betting each way is when you have a sneaky fancy for a horse at long odds but doubt, in reality, whether the bet will be successful. This sounds a bit weird because I will talk shortly of the need to have a rational basis for betting, and thinking that a bet is unlikely to succeed doesn't sound the best reason for making it. However, this can happen and it ties in with the idea of value, which I'll also discuss later.

In some races (nearly always high-level non-handicaps), the 'market' will become obsessed about just a couple of horses in the race – there may be talk of two horses, perhaps the apparent champions of two generations, 'going head to head' and so on. It may very well be that one or other is the most likely winner, but often virtually everyone will back these horses, forcing their odds to contract, while those of the rest of the field lengthen. At this point, some shrewd punters may back a couple of other runners at what seem attractive odds, so their odds may also start to shorten and the remaining runners will 'go for a walk in the market'. Sometimes, when this happens, a horse who has pretty decent form and is worthy of his place in the line-up may end up at very generous odds.

As with human sportsmen and athletes, there is often not much between horses at the top of the tree and, although logic may suggest (often rightly) that horses A and B are pretty likely to beat horse C, it doesn't require much to alter in order to upset expectations. For example, if one of the top fancies usually benefits from a **pacemaker**, and the pacemaker doesn't do his job, that can change the tactical shape of the race. It may be that one of the reasonably well-fancied runners doesn't, for some reason, run his race. It may be that the horse for whom you have a sneaky fancy is particularly well suited by soft ground, whereas other, better fancied, runners are not, and there has been a morning's unexpected deluge.

Other than the last reason, those just given are, before the actual event, pure specula-tion, but they *do* sometimes happen. The point is that sometimes a horse may end up at a *much* longer price than you think his form merits. That *does not* materially improve his chances, but it can make a small each way bet worth doing because, for the price of a pint of beer, there is the chance that you might spend the rest of the day feeling smug and having a few quid in your pocket.

A couple of months before writing this, I had a small each way bet on a mare in a top-class mile race. I didn't remotely believe that she could win the race – I speculated that, if she ran up to her best, she was likely to finish just behind the placed horses – but I was unconvinced about a couple of other runners and she was on offer at 66–1. At half those odds, I wouldn't have thought of backing her, but this price was *so* long it seemed worth a small interest. In the event, she was run out of third place by a neck, in the last few strides. Of course, this was a losing bet, so it's hard to argue with anyone who says it was not worthwhile. However, in terms of *nearly* having my judgement proved right, it was worth doing, for a small sum, for interest. I have done similar things in the past and have backed placed horses at odds as long as this, and you don't need many of them to think it's worth doing once in a while, *if you do really have a bit of a fancy for the horse*, but keep your expectations modest. Certainly, with bets of this sort, each way is the way to go.

Each Way Considerations

With each way bets, there is a cut-off point at which they aren't really worth doing, because the basic odds of the horse are too short. Earlier, I said that it may well be worth backing a horse each way at odds of 9–2 because, so long as he was placed, you would more or less recover the lost 'win' part of your bet. However, if the odds are much shorter than this, the 'place' element returns so little that you have to ask yourself whether it's worthwhile. Suppose, for example, you put £5 each way on a horse at 2–1, and he was just placed. At one-fifth of the odds, you would get back a total of £7, which is better than losing £10, but perhaps getting towards the point when you wonder whether it was worth bothering with bet of this nature.

Place Only Bets

With a pool system, while it is possible to have a pool version of an each way bet, it is also possible to have a place only bet. This will pay out on a horse who is 'placed' in the context of the specific race (see 'Placed and Place Odd' above). As mentioned there, 'being placed' includes winning, but with a place only bet the dividend will be the same regardless of whether the horse wins or is otherwise placed.

Since, with a pool system, there is a separate pool for place bets, this means that such bets are not tied to being a set proportion of the 'win' odds, as is the case with an each way bet with a bookie. Because, with a place only bet, you don't have to add in the possibly losing 'win' part of the each way bet, some people who think their fancy is more likely to make the frame than win will bet place only with a pool system, and this can mean that place payouts from the pool may be lower than the each way element of a bookie's bet – although this will vary on a race by race basis. However, in comparing the financial outcome of the two types of bet you have to factor in the losing cost of the 'win' part of an each way bet with a bookie. Depending on the place terms for the individual race (usually a fifth or a quarter of the odds), an each way bet with a bookie, in which the horse was just placed, would have to be at odds of at least 4–1 (commonly 5–1) to break even; a successful place only pool bet will always deliver *some* profit, whilst also avoiding any lost 'win' element.

Since, with pool betting, it is possible to bet both 'win only' and 'place only' you have, if you wish, the facility to adjust your bet to cover your options in a way that you can't do with a straight each way bet. If, for instance, you thought your fancy was pretty likely to be placed, but had only a small chance of winning, you could have, say, a bigger place bet and a smaller win bet.

THOUGHTS ON BETTING

The ideas within this section won't necessarily make your betting successful, but they may help to reduce losses arising from irrational bets and provide some rationale for those you do place. (It is somehow easier to accept a losing bet if you have some idea why you made it, than if it was a random act aimed mainly at lightening your wallet.)

Financial Prudence

The first point that I'd like to hammer home is that betting is entirely voluntary and if you don't enjoy it, or wish to do it, then don't. Clearly, you can't lose money if you don't bet (although you can't win any, either). The second point is that, if you bet, do so in properly affordable amounts and, if you're having a losing day, don't start 'chasing your losses' by betting more than is prudent on the remaining races in an attempt to win your money back. However, there is a kind of corollary to this that says you shouldn't let previous losses put you off backing a horse you genuinely fancy in a later race, *provided you're betting within your means*, because your choice of horses in earlier races will not influence the result of a later one. Also, if you're having a winning day, it may be worthwhile increasing your normal stake on a later race a *little* if you *really* fancy the horse, because you will be betting out of your profit. Nonetheless, it still makes sense to be prudent – perhaps if your normal bet is a fiver, you may choose to risk a tenner because, if this horse wins, you will have made the day better by some margin and if he loses, you will probably still be ahead on the day. Of course, if you lump all your profit on and the horse wins, things will look very rosy but, if he loses, you will be back to square one and probably feeling pretty deflated. It is a good idea not to be greedy or overconfident.

Choosing Races

If you follow the fortunes of top racing columnists/tipsters in the press you will find that,

Betting Questions

Never ask yourself: 'What shall I back in this race?' Instead, ask: 'Is there a horse in this race I fancy?' Then, if the answer is 'yes', ask yourself 'why?'

while they can have some very good days with their selections of horses, overall, a lot of the horses they tip don't win. One very obvious reason for this is that sometimes they just get things wrong. Another reason is that, as part of their job, they are more or less obliged to offer a selection for every race. No matter how diligent and well-informed they may be, they cannot realistically be familiar with the form of every horse in every race. Even if they *were* familiar with the individual form of all the horses in a race, sometimes there might be little if anything in terms of relative form (previous form of one runner against another, or a link via a third party) and, even where there *is* relative form, it doesn't always work out, for a whole variety of perfectly legitimate reasons. The fact that these racing professionals select a lot of losers should convey the message to us mere mortals that trying to pick the winner of every race is – let's say – unwise.

I have followed racing closely for nearly fifty years and am very happy to watch with interest all sorts of races in which I haven't the first clue who will be the likely winner. Sometimes, races such as this will throw up a horse worth keeping an eye on for the future and sometimes a horse I've decided at the last minute to watch may win, without the weight of my money to slow him down. However, this doesn't happen all the time and if, in the lead-up to the race, your considered opinion is 'haven't a clue', the sensible reaction is to keep your wallet tightly shut.

It's not easy to give definitive guidance about races to avoid for betting purposes but, in general, it is worth being wary of the following:

- Races where few horses have any previous form – a prime example being early-season two-year-old races on the flat. There may be little relative form between those runners who have any form at all, and even the most experienced trainers are sometimes surprised (for better or worse) by how a runner will cope with the day and perform on the track.
- Moderate races where none of the runners have eye-catching form figures – often selling races (*see* Chapter 2) and suchlike. There may be reasons of soundness or temperament issues to explain horses' past performances, or they may just not be any good as racehorses.
- Ultra-competitive races where, with the best will in the world, you can't figure out a reason to prefer one horse over the others. (If you can, there's no reason not to have a modest interest, but don't go looking for a horse to back just because it's the Derby/Grand National/whatever.)

Choosing Horses

If you are going to back a horse, do it for a reason that has some rationale behind it – by which I mean some evidence that suggests he could run well. This may seem rather obvious, but some people who bet on horses give reasons that clearly have no bearing on the horse's chances – for example neither the horse's name, nor his jockey's colours, nor his coat colour* will improve his prospects.

---

* Further to this, some people like to bet on greys and they do, usually, have the advantage that these horses are easy to spot in a race. However, they will be on the horns of a considerable dilemma if they visit Newmarket on the day that the course runs its 'greys only' race – I suppose the choice then is either to back every horse in the race or revert to sticking a pin in, neither of which is recommended.

Of course, a bet having some rationale behind it does not guarantee success, but when such bets do come in, the fact that you were 'proved right' perhaps adds to the satisfaction and (even if there's no financial difference) they must surely be more satisfying than a 'random' selection that happened to come in, like a lucky bet at roulette.

So, what decisions might be considered to have a rationale behind them? For a newcomer to racing, this is harder to answer than it would be for a regular race-goer, with a lot of knowledge about many of the horses, trainers, jockeys, course character-istics and so on.

In the previous chapter we saw that a good deal of information can be gleaned from a racecard and, although this may be subject to interpretation, there are still some prag-matic basics that can be gleaned from it to help you form a view about the runners. The following are a few to bear in mind.

- If a horse has shown no previous evidence that he will be suited by the distance or ground conditions of the race in question, these are 'unknowns' at best and not positive reasons for putting money on him. Similarly, if there is evidence that he's previously run poorly at the course, this should be seen as a negative. Of course, none of these things *necessarily* mean that the horse won't run well – connections may have their reasons for trying a new distance or running him on different ground or, when he ran poorly on a previous occasion he might have been off-colour – but these issues would only be apparent after the event and you can't bet retrospect-ively.
- In jumping races, no horse is going to win if he doesn't complete the course, so there is a significant risk involved in backing horses with more than the odd letter (P, U, F – *see* Chapter 5) in their form figures. This is not to say that such horses can't or don't win in some circumstances, but it is hardly an encouragement to put money on them. Ask yourself the question: 'Why am I thinking of backing this horse?' and see whether you can answer: 'Because he seems to jump badly' or: 'Because he seems to have a problem with finishing his races', with any real enthusiasm.
- As we saw in the previous chapter, there is more to form figures than just what they say on the racecard but, even on a superficial level, they can provide the *beginning* of a rationale about whether it is worth looking further into a horse's past perform-ances or, perhaps, not. As I said in that chapter, a horse with impressive-looking form figures may not always have a better chance in a race than one whose figures look less impressive, because there will be other factors to take into account. That said, a horse with a series of wins and/or near misses against his name has at least proved that he is able to get 'in the mix' consistently and that consideration (even it were trumped in the race by other criteria) does give some rationale for considering whether to back him. If, in answer to: 'Why did I back that horse' you can say: 'He seemed a consistent type who kept finishing thereabouts,' that answer would seem more rational than: 'Because he never seems to have been involved in the finish of any races lately.'
- One issue that surfaces from time to time when racing presenters interview race-goers is an apparent tendency to back jockeys, rather than horses (when asked who they've backed, the race-goer gives the jockey's name). If this is a genuine choice, it makes little sense, for the fairly obvious reason that it is the horse, not the jockey, who is doing the running.

I have great admiration for jockeys and am permanently surprised and disappointed by the fact that their skills seem under-appreciated (and often misunderstood) by riders in the other equestrian disciplines. A top jockey is likely to be an asset to any horse, and a jockey who has shown a special tactical talent for riding a particular course (there are various examples) or a particularly quirky horse is likewise a bonus. However, even though jockeys may sometimes have a purple patch, it is a fact that the majority of horses ridden even by champion jockeys don't win. Jockeys, either by retained contract or individual arrangement, ride pretty much every horse they're asked to ride, and most of these horses will be incapable of winning the races in which they are running. A top jockey may be able to get a horse to perform to the very best of his ability, but no jockey can get a horse to gallop faster than he is physically capable of doing. Therefore, if a horse you fancy has the benefit of a top jockey on board, consider this a bonus, but it makes little sense to simply 'back a jockey' unless you intend to run onto the course to give him a piggy back to the finish.

· Another tendency among some race-goers is to back a horse just because he's the favourite or *just because* he's an outsider. In both cases there is a rationale of sorts, but it is unrelated to the backer's assessment of the actual horse.

In the former case, it is a decision based on other people's opinion (i.e. those who have put money on the horse), but putting money on a horse doesn't actually make him run any better. Of course, a number of favourites *do* win – but many don't, which makes the point that the market often get things wrong. Furthermore, by definition, the favourite is always the horse at the shortest odds (except when he is co-favourite, and thus one of the horses at shortest odds) so returns, even on winning favourites, are fairly modest. That, of itself, is no reason not to back a winning favourite – it's a better outcome than backing a losing long shot – but the risk/reward element becomes muddied when really short prices are involved. A bet is termed '**odds on**' when you have to risk more to back the horse than you win if he does – for example if he is two to one on (usually written 1–2), you have to put £10 on him to win £5 (i.e. get £15 back) and, unless you are a risk-taker betting in considerable sums (which I don't advise) this is hardly worth doing and not much fun. When writing these lines, I looked at random at the weekday results from three race meetings (a total of eighteen races) and saw that two odds-on favourites had been beaten that day.

My view about favourites is that, if you really fancy a horse, the fact that he is favourite shouldn't put you off but, alternately, you shouldn't back a horse *just because* he's favourite. Also, you should consider whether his odds as favourite represent value – a point we'll look at below.

The converse of backing favourites is backing outsiders because 'I'll get a lot of money if he wins'. That is true, so far as it goes and outsiders do sometimes win, but not with great frequency. Also, if you are just looking to back 'an outsider' for the odds, rather than a specific horse, which do you choose, and why? Betting like this is getting into the realms of buying lucky dip cards at the local minimarket. You might strike lucky on occasion, but how many cards did you have to buy first? In my view, if you are going to back an outsider, do so because you have reason to believe that he may well outrun his odds, not just because of the odds in isolation. This point brings us on to the consideration of value, which is something that can be applied usefully to all bets.

Value

When looking at horses' odds with a view to perhaps placing a bet, one import-ant consideration is what regular punters call 'value'. This, essentially, is about form-ing an opinion as to whether it's worthwhile placing a bet on a particular horse at the current odds. In principle, this is something that people who like a little flutter may do in various scenarios in other sports and games: here is an example from the game of golf.

Suppose you are a golfer of fair ability playing your normal course with a friend. Coming to the easiest hole on the course, he bets you a fiver you won't par it, or better. This is a hole that you par fairly frequently so, although there are no guarantees, you say: 'Okay, you're on.' Although this is an **even money** bet (you either win or lose the fiver), what value there is lies that in the fact that there's a fairly good chance you'll succeed, and the bet is modest. Now suppose you were coming to a really long, difficult par 5, a hole you rarely par and have birdied only once, by holing a fluky bunker shot. Your friend says: 'I bet you £100 you can't birdie this hole.' Now, although the money would come in handy, and although you *have* done this once, you rarely get anywhere near doing so and, while it is again an even money bet, you don't fancy losing that kind of money. There is clearly no value in this bet at all. But what if your friend says: 'I'll give you odds of £100 to £1 that you can't birdie this hole?' Now things are different. It is still very unlikely that you'll succeed, but you have done it in the past and now you are risking only £1 with the (very slight) chance of winning £100. At these odds, it may well be worth the risk.

This may be a fairly crude illustration but, at its heart, it is making the point that, before placing a bet, it is a good idea to ask yourself: 'Is it worth it?'

The way that experienced racing punters approach this issue is to form a view of the price they themselves think a horse should be. (Obviously, they do this after consider-ation of the factors that, in their view, influence his chances.) If, for instance, they expect a horse should be about 6–1, they are likely to bet at that price, but if the horse is, say 4–1 or shorter, they will probably consider this poor value, and may refrain from betting. Note that, of *itself*, this price differential has no material effect on the horse's chances and the reaction of some people to the shorter odds may be: 'Oh, he's really fancied – I'd better put a bet on before the odds shorten more.' The reaction of more experienced punters to price variations can be almost the opposite of this: the experienced punter expecting 6–1 is likely to be happy if the horse is priced at 7–1 or 8–1 and will almost certainly place a bet because it is seen as 'good value', although there may be some constraints to this latter course of action in some circumstances. If, for instance, a horse is a short price to begin with, because it is reasonable to assume from past perform-ances that he has a very good chance, and his price starts to get *appreciably* longer, this may be a sign that people in the know have concerns about his well-being. (I'm not talking here about dodgy practices, but about matters such as the horse not seem-ing to have worked well in the past few days, evidence that some horses in the same yard are coughing, and suchlike.) In situations like this, people may either (rightly or wrongly) see warning signs and not place the bet, or chance the possibility that any rumours are ill-founded, and consider that the favourable price represents a worth-while risk.

To evaluate specific races in the way that experienced punters do will, to a large extent, require quite a bit of knowledge about the horses involved, but even without this, there are some broad guidelines worth considering, which relate to points touched upon earlier.

- If the race is for inexperienced horses, with little in the way of previous form, it will probably not be the best race to bet on anyway, but there is not much 'value' in backing a horse who is a short price. Although connections may have strong grounds for fancying the horse (on the basis of his work at home, etc.), there is not much value at backing him at, say 6–4. If you decline to do so he may, of course, win 'in a canter' (in which case, remember you haven't lost), but it's also possible that he may dwell in the stalls, **run green** in the closing stages and get beaten by a head by a 20–1 shot or, in a novice NH race, fall at the first, or whatever.
- In handicaps with big fields, a hot favourite may well be bad value. Remember, handicaps are *supposed* to give every horse in the race an even chance (even if, despite the official handicapper's best efforts, things rarely pan out like this) so, if one horse is at significantly shorter odds than any of the others, this might be because a lot of people have got excited about his recent form and rather ignored the form of others in the race. Although hot favourites *do* win some big handicaps, they quite often don't, and taking a short price against a horse with, say, twenty opponents, can rarely be considered good value.
- In a race in which you definitely fancy a runner, but realize that there are several others who also have fairly evident chances, the value option may well be each way or place betting (as discussed earlier). Provided that the odds make this viable, it increases the chances of coming out of the race with a small profit (or a reduced loss), whereas a win only bet would be 'sink or swim'.

When Gut Instinct Kicks In

Although, in this chapter, I have stressed the importance of prudent, rational betting, there is one issue on which I would take a short step away from this stance. If you are someone who does bet, then it's worth listening to those occasional surges of 'gut instinct' that seem to affect us all at times, in respect of all sorts of issues. Therefore, if you get a *real* feeling about some horse, it is worth having a bet on him – albeit perhaps a small one – because, if you don't, and he wins, it will be *very* irritating. (If he loses, you can console yourself with the thought that the modest outlay was an insurance policy against the feeling of self-loathing you'd have experienced had he won, unbacked by you.)

PS: written shortly after *not backing* a 25–1 winner, who made all the running.

Forecasts and Multiple Bets

These bets involve backing more than one horse in various ways, and range from fairly simple to massively complex. Since it is hard enough to pick one winner, I'm not going to discuss these bets in great detail, but will concentrate on a basic explanation of the simpler forms. The more complex ones generally expand on the principles underlying the simpler ones. Course bookies don't commonly take these bets, but High Street shops take most of them and pool systems have their own versions.

Forecasts involve predicting the finishing order of horses in a single race, the simplest being naming the winner and the second in correct order. This is called a straight forecast and is a single bet. Winning bets with High Street bookies are paid to a sum calculated by computer (computer straight forecast or CSF), the calculation being based on the individual odds of the horses involved, the number of runners and various other factors. The longer the odds of the horses, the higher the return should be. Returns on these bets are stated decimally, to a £1 unit, and include the stake, so if you place a £3 forecast and the CSF is 9.2, you get back £27.60.

A reverse forecast is a way of saying that you want to back horse A to win while horse B comes second, and vice versa, so it is really two straight forecasts, and thus two bets (one of which is bound to lose, unless these two horses dead-heat). As two bets, a £3 reverse forecast will cost £6 and, if one of the combinations wins, you will be paid out on that basis.

A tricast bet is an expanded version of a forecast requiring that you name the winner, second and third horses in the correct order. Although it is clearly possible to do this, it is by no means easy, and it could be frustrating (to say the least) to pick out the first three and place them as 1, 3, 2 in a tricast. A combination tricast (six bets naming the three horses in the possible finishing orders) avoids that possibility, but means six lost bets if one horse fails to finish in the first three.

Multiple bets are bets linking different horses in different races, done at the same time in the form of one compound bet. These really need to be worked out at home, or on a train to the races, and placed in a bookie's shop, or with a pool system, as appropriate. The simplest multiple is a win double linking, for example, a horse in the 2 o'clock at Plumpton with one in the 3 o'clock at Haydock. In this scenario you could, of course, back the horse in the earlier race then, depending on the outcome, put some or all of your winnings on the horse in the later race or, if you lose on the first race, make a new choice about whether to bet on the second race, and the amount to put on – although these actions would require another visit to the bookie. With a win double, you are telling the bookie in a compound bet that you want to put your stake on the 2 o'clock horse and, if he wins, you want *all* your winnings (stake included) to go on the 3 o'clock horse. If, for example, the horse's odds are 2–1 and 5–1, and you place a £10 bet (and both win) the arithmetic is: £10 at 2–1 = £30 (inc. stake) at 5–1 = £180 return. However, if the first horse loses, you have no stake to go on the second horse – you lose, regardless of how the second horse performs.

You can use the same principle to link three horses (a treble) or four or more (an accumulator) if you so wish, but bear in mind that, as with single win bets, if one horse loses, the whole bet is lost. Just to drive this point home, if you placed a £2 win accumulator on horses at 3–1, 5–1, 4–1 and 8–1 and the first three all won, you would have £240 going on the 8–1 horse, which would be great if he won, but less so if he didn't. (Some online firms now allow you to 'cash out' a multiple bet if your nerve goes after the initial winners – i.e. take your winnings to that point and run – but that is not something I intend to deal with here.)

You can, of course, do all these bets each way, which will increase your chances of some return, but it is important to understand how this works. For instance, referring back to the example just given, as long as your 8–1 loser was placed, you would still make a reasonable profit from the place part of your bet but, if this horse was unplaced then, despite having three winners, the whole bet would lose.

The way that place returns on each way multiples work out is that place terms (dependent on the number of runners in each race), will apply to that part of the bet. In the example of the 2–1 and 5–1 double given earlier, if the bet was £10 *each way*, in addition to the £180 win part, you will (assuming a fifth of the odds for the place) get back a sum calculated as follows: 2–1 at one-fifth of the odds becomes two-fifths of £10 = £4, which, plus your original stake, becomes £14 going on the 5–1 horse which, at one-fifth of the odds becomes 1–1, hence you win another £14, which means you get a return of £28 on the place bet.

As with the win part of the bet, if either horse fails to get placed, the bet is lost. This means that you need to be careful about how many runners there are in all races in which you place multiple bets. Suppose, for example, that the first horse was second in a seven-horse race, and the second horse was third, also in a seven-horse race. While the first horse was placed, the second one, under normal betting terms, was not (he would have been, had there been eight or more runners, but there weren't, so you lose).

The other point to note about doubles (and other multiples), is that if one horse wins, but the other is only placed, the win part of the whole bet fails. To give an extreme example, if you placed a six-horse each way accumulator and five of the horses won but the other came second, only the each way element of the whole bet would count.

Because, with these straightforward accumulative bets, one loser (or unplaced horse) will cause the bet to fail, it is worth mentioning a couple of other multiple-type bets from which you can still get a return if this happens. The first is called a patent, and it links three horses from different races as three single bets, three doubles, and one treble – thus it requires seven units (e.g. a £1 win patent costs £7). If all three horses win, then all seven bets win, which can be quite lucrative. If any two horses win, then you have two winning single bets, and one winning double. If just one horse wins, you have just one winning bet but, supposing that horse was just 3–1, you still get more than half of your £7 back.

A more complex multiple bet is a Yankee, which links four horses from different races in the following way – six doubles, four trebles and a four-horse accumulator in eleven bets (thus a £1 Yankee costs £11). Although the potential rewards can be considerable if all the horses win, you will see that, to get any return, you need a minimum of two winners (i.e. one double), while three winners will get you three doubles and one treble. Reverting to the observation that it's hard enough to find one winner, getting the maximum benefit from a Yankee is quite a task.

It is perfectly possible to bet each way on both patents and Yankees, but this does mean doubling the number of bets required, which, unless you bet in very small units, may be a case of stepping out of your comfort zone.

The Tote does offer two multiple bets to a small (£2) stake, that many people find attractive, although the former is perhaps best viewed mainly as an intellectual challenge, a bit like doing a difficult cryptic crossword in a foreign language. This is the scoop6, which requires you to pick the winners of six designated races (a couple of which are likely to be almost impenetrable) on a Saturday. Its little brother, called the placepot, requires you to pick horses to be placed in the first six races on the card, which is more likely to be achievable. Although there's no harm in trying these for fun, one significant drawback is that they are highly likely to require you to try to pick horses in some races you otherwise wouldn't consider as betting mediums.

With multiple bets generally, it is perhaps wisest to leave them for those occasions when you really strongly fancy several horses and have backed them individually. Then, if you feel so inclined, you can couple them in a small-stakes multiple 'just in case'.

Collecting Your Winnings

Collecting any winnings should be pretty straightforward. If your bet was with the Tote, you just go to the 'pay' window and present your ticket.* With a bookie (whether racecourse or High Street) you do the same with your betting slip. It makes sense to collect any winnings promptly (and you will doubtless wish to do so), but if you temporarily mislay your ticket, or have to leave the course because of an emergency, that doesn't necessarily mean that any chance of getting paid out is lost. The AGT has procedures in place for dealing with lost/unclaimed tickets issued by course bookmakers (*see* www.agt-ltd.co.uk). High Street bookies will keep their copies of winning slips readily on hand to pay out for some days after the race in question, but in due course will place these bets into a 'sleeper' pile. This doesn't mean they won't honour any winnings, but it can mean faffing about for all concerned, so it makes sense to collect any winnings within a few days. If you have actually lost a betting slip, it is worth talking to the shop manager because, if you can describe your bet accurately, he may be able to assist.

An important point to remember in connection with writing multiple bets on one slip in a High Street shop is that in addition to 'winnings' you need to consider 'returns'. The former term suggests that you are going to get back more than you laid out, but sometimes you will have returns (money to come back on a betting slip) despite it being less than you laid out. Suppose, in the example given earlier in this chapter (Principles of Betting with Bookmakers) where your bets totalled £14, both Roadhump and Petrified were unplaced, but Turned To Stone won at 5–4, you would have £9 to collect. Something similar can also happen if you've had just one each way bet (whether in a shop or with an on-course bookie), and the horse has been placed at fairly short odds. For example, at one-fifth of the odds, a £5 each way bet at 4–1 will leave you with £9 to collect.

Also, remember that if you back a horse on the day of the race and he is a non-runner, your stake will be refunded.

---

* The Tote's practice has been to pay out on a valid ticket at any of their outlets (i.e. not necessarily the venue where the bet was placed). It may be that similar arrangements are envisaged for other pool systems, but details are unclear at the time of writing.

Other Forms of Betting

Many readers may be aware that it is possible to bet online and via mobile apps, and with betting exchanges. This is not something I do personally. I will simply say that the principles and thought process behind betting remain relevant, regardless of the medium in which bets are placed.

CHAPTER 7

Watching a Race

Actually watching the racing is really what a day at the races should be about. Clearly, if you've had a bet, there is a powerful incentive to follow the progress of your fancy, but, whether you've done so or not, concentrated viewing can provide you with all sorts of information as to how various horses perform (perhaps useful for a bet on another occasion) and it will draw you more closely into the multi-sensual experience of colour, sound and speed associated with a field of horses galloping flat out.

The watching process begins well before a race actually starts and, depending on the layout of the individual course and your own mobility, you should be able to take in several aspects of each one. This chapter offers guidance about what you can observe from different parts of the course – for maximum interest and to understand more about the sport, it is a good idea to get 'up close and personal' from different viewpoints as and when the mood takes you.

IN THE PADDOCK

Horses will usually be made ready for a race in the saddling boxes, which are not normally open to the public. They may then be walked briefly round a pre-parade ring to check that all is in order, before being taken to the paddock (which is, itself, sometimes referred to as 'the parade ring') where they will again be walked around for a few minutes, while the jockeys emerge from the **weighing room** to meet owners and trainers and receive last-minute instructions, before mounting and heading out onto the course.

Time Flies

When you first go racing and realize that the normal gap between races is thirty minutes (sometimes a little more at big meetings) this may seem like a long time – although, for those actively involved in the races – the officials, trainers, stable staff and jockeys it is anything but. In practice, this time will also pass for you much more quickly than you imagine. There are, of course, the essentials of life to deal with – trips to the loo, the bar, the food outlets and, hopefully, to the bookie to collect your winnings from the previous race – but it will soon be time to peruse the racecard to check out the runners in the next race, and it won't be long before they start to appear in the paddock.

Before a big race, there will be a lot of attention on horses in the saddling boxes.

Groups of connections awaiting their horses in the paddock.

Some horses get their own supporters' club.

Observing the Horses

The period of walking around before being mounted serves as a gentle warming up/ stretching for the horses before they canter to the start, and provides an opportunity for race-goers to assess the horses' appearance and demeanour. Experienced race-goers can make quite useful judgements about the horses at this point, although this does require considerable knowledge of horses in general and individuals in particular (*see* note on conformation in Chapter 8). That said, the following can be helpful pointers in making a decision about whether or not you wish to go ahead and back a horse whose form in the racecard caught your attention.

If you have no pre-knowledge of a particular horse, signs that can usually be considered positive include a bright, shiny coat (although this may be less evident on a misty day in February – and the coat may only be visible for a brief period when the rug is taken off), a free-and-easy, but purposeful, regular walk and a generally calm disposition. A horse who is clearly 'playing up' – prancing around, barging his handler and perhaps kicking out – is obviously using up energy before it is necessary to do so and may therefore be inclined to be too **free to post**, and perhaps hard to settle during the race itself. This does not necessarily mean that he can't win, but he is not helping his cause. If a horse starts to sweat up in the paddock, showing visible sweat underneath the saddle and/or between the hind legs, this again is not a good sign, because it is indicative of nervous tension. (Minor patches of sweat on the neck/shoulder can usually

In cooler weather, horses' rugs will be kept on until the jockeys are ready to mount, which is good for the horses, but reduces the time available for physical assessment.

Horses with a long-striding, easy walk often move well in their faster gaits. This photo was taken at a stable's open day, but similar movement in a racecourse paddock will catch the eye.

Sometimes the presence of two handlers can help keep a horse calm in the paddock.

be ignored on a hot, humid day.) However, this is an example of where it is useful to know a horse's previous history. Some horses do, habitually, sweat up before racing and, if this is the case, the sweaty individual may still run up to his normal level of form. (This is one of many examples of the fact that racing involves living, breathing creatures who need to be understood as individuals. Sweating like this can never *help* a horse and, if he didn't do it, he would probably be slightly better but, if it is part of 'who he is' it may not prevent him from being a good, consistent performer. Furthermore, the connections of such a horse may be more concerned if he *doesn't* sweat before a race because, although this could be a welcome sign that he is maturing and calming down, the simple change in habitual characteristics might also be an early indication that he is not feeling quite himself.)

Further to excitement and past experience, sometimes a horse will be accompanied by not one handler, but two. This may indicate that he has been 'wound up' in the paddock on an earlier occasion, or that connections are concerned about the likelihood of him becoming so but, in most cases, the extra attention seems to work pretty well as a 'belt and braces' measure, and the horse remains reasonably well behaved. However, if circumstances permit, it can be informative to see how such a horse goes on to conduct himself on the way to the start – whether he canters down sensibly or gives his jockey a bit of a hard time.

Regarding horses who get 'wound up', it is useful to learn how to distinguish between signs of temperament and adrenalin-overload as distinct from signs that a horse is simply 'up for it'. Those who follow human sports, such as athletics and boxing, for example, may have an instinct for this that they can transpose into watching horses. In simple terms, horses who seem erratic and fidgety in their movement, who look wild-eyed and move in a stilted fashion with a high **head-carriage** and 'concave' outline of their upper body, are likely to be dissipating nervous energy. Those who seem to be checking out their surroundings with interest, ears pricked, walking forward rhythmically or perhaps breaking occasionally into a few fluent strides of trot, before settling back to walk, are the ones who most readily suggest that it might be worth checking out their current odds.

That said, while a horse who looks keen and alert, yet basically composed, will always catch the eye, the fact that another horse appears to be plodding around half asleep is *not necessarily* a negative. Some individuals – including some very good horses – are remarkably laidback in the preliminaries, which helps conserve all their nervous energy for the race itself. Again, knowledge of what is normal for the individual can be helpful here because, seen in an individual who is usually a 'live wire' in the paddock, such signs may suggest that something is amiss. With all the regular health checks undertaken by trainers nowadays, plus the veterinary support available both off- and on-course, it would be very unusual now to see a snotty nose in the paddock, or to hear a cough but, if either were evident, this would be a clear signal not to back the individual concerned.

All the runners in this steeplechase have additional equipment of some sort. All are wearing breastgirths, two have sheepskin nosebands and the other three have cross nosebands. The horse in green and yellow colours is wearing a hood. These items are explained in the main text that follows.

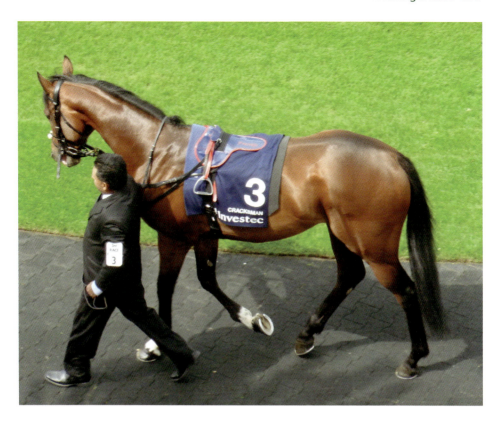

A good illustration of the size of saddle often used by jockeys. This is a very light example being used by a jockey in a flat race.

Horses' Equipment

One other point to note when viewing horses in the paddock is the equipment they are wearing. This can give some indication as to their racing characteristics and may also help you to identify your fancy in a crowded field during the race itself. The basic equipment, in which many horses run, is simply a saddle and a bridle, with reins and bit. There are, however, a number of additions/variations to this basic kit, which can either be pointers to a horse's likely character and running style or, at least, help to identify him during the race. The following are some variations of equipment that you may notice, with brief explanations of their purpose.

Saddle   All racing saddles are of markedly different design compared with ordinary riding saddles, one key point being that they are designed for riders galloping with very short stirrup leathers. The other key point is that they are vastly lighter than traditional saddles. If a jockey weighs several pounds less than the weight at which he is required to ride, he will probably make up some of the difference by using a (relatively) big saddle – by which I mean one weighing just a few pounds – rather than putting weights in his weight cloth. However, if he is riding at close to his minimum weight, he will use a really light saddle. With the advent of modern, hi-tech materials, these saddles, known as 'postage stamps', may weigh just 1lb or so, or even a little less, and really just provide something to perch on and a place on which to attach the stirrup leathers and irons.

Breastgirth   Fit racehorses are necessarily fairly lean and some are particularly so as a product of their natural conformation. Particularly with the latter, there can be a possibility that, during a race as their body tightens up, the girth, which normally holds the saddle in place, will cease to do so efficiently and the saddle may start to slip backwards. Although this can happen in flat races, the jumping effort in NH races can add to the likelihood. Therefore, if there is a concern that this might happen, the horse may be fitted with a breastgirth, a strap fastened to the saddle and around the horse's chest, as a preventative measure.

The metal rings through which the reins run below this horse's neck are the rings of an Irish martingale.

Irish martingale   Those familiar with other forms of riding will be aware that martingales in various designs are intended to prevent a horse from raising his head above a desirable level, and will rightly conclude that this device, despite its name, can have no such function. It is simply a short leather strap, with a ring at each end, through which the reins run beneath a horse's neck, hence the more descriptive name 'a pair of spectacles'. Although it has some function in maintaining any pull on the reins in a correct direction (which could be helpful if a rider became seriously unbalanced) its main purpose in racing is to reduce the chance of the reins coming over the horse's head in the event of the fall, and thus reduce the chance of the horse trapping a foreleg in them. This being their function, these devices are quite often seen on jumping horses.

Bridle modifications   The following are fairly common variations from/additions to the standard form of bridle.

Australian cheeker   This device, typically made of orange rubber (but sometimes other colours) runs down the horse's face and divides into two sections, through which the bit rings protrude. It lifts the bit a little in the horse's mouth, and helps to keep it still. Partly by its mechanical action and perhaps partly by psychological effect, it may have some restraining effect on free-running horses. Some trainers use this devices on quite a few of their runners. From the race-goer's perspective, it is a piece of equipment that may help identify a runner.

The rubber device running down this horse's nose and dividing into two is called a cheeker. It helps hold the bit still in the horse's mouth. Some trainers fit this to a lot of their charges.

Dark Horses; Bright Bridles

Most bridles and reins are made of leather, with rubber grips on the reins to assist the jockeys. However, a few trainers run their horses in bridles made of artificial material, which has no effect on the horse's performance but may assist identification during a race, since these are usually white in colour – or very occasionally dayglo colours, which may make the horse a target for the fashion police. (The jockey can plead: 'Nothing to do with me mate, I'm just riding it.')

Grakle or cross noseband   This noseband was devised for the winner of the 1931 Grand National and is commonly misspelt 'Grackle' by people unaware of the fact. It is a figure-of-eight shape, crossing over the horse's face, usually at a padded junction, and fastening below the bit. It is intended to increase control of strong horses, so those wearing such a noseband are likely to be instinctively **keen** runners.

This horse is wearing cheekpieces and a cross noseband called a Grakle, after the Grand National winner for whom it was first designed.

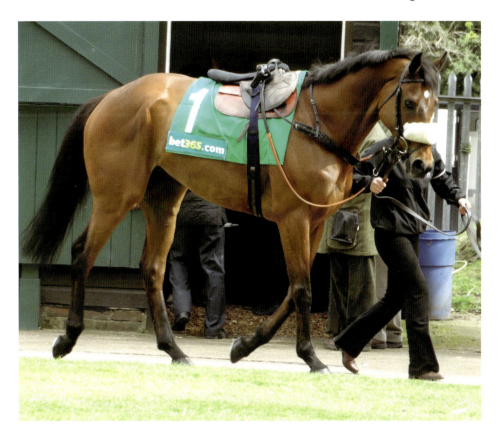

This horse is wearing a breastgirth, a sheepskin noseband and an (obscured) cross noseband.

Sheepskin noseband   This piece of equipment consists of a thick piece of sheepskin fitted to the noseband that lies across the horse's face a little above the nostrils. The idea behind it is that it would, to a degree, interfere with the horse's vision if he raised his head undesirably high, so fitting it encourages him to race in an outline that is mechanically efficient from his point of view and assists the jockey to keep him controlled and balanced. Some trainers fit these nosebands to most of their charges. A bonus for the race-goer is that these nosebands are usually white(ish), which can aid identification of the wearer – although some are dyed to match the main shade of the owner's colours.

Bit variations   The purpose of a bit, in any form of equitation, is to assist the rider to control the horse's forward movement and steering. To achieve this to best effect, the horse must be comfortable in the bit and happy to 'move into the rider's hands' while still respecting the action of the bit. From a racing perspective, this means that, while the jockey must be able to control the horse at a fast gallop, this must not be at the expense of the horse being unwilling to race enthusiastically (go 'into the bridle'). The type of bit used on most racehorses is called a snaffle, which will be typified by more or less round rings on the outside of the horse's lips. Occasionally, in addition to the rings, you will see bars, called 'cheeks', extending upwards and downwards from the rings or

Horse number 6 is wearing a snaffle bit with 'cheeks'. The white colour of the mouthpiece suggests that it is nylon, which in turn suggests that he has a sensitive mouth.

This horse is wearing a Dexter ring bit – a design becoming increasingly popular in racing. It looks rather strange, but many horses who wear it seem to go kindly in it.

the ends of the bit mouthpiece. This pattern is sometimes used to keep a bit in position in a horse's mouth if his steering is not as good as it might be, perhaps because he lacks balance or is just a bit 'awkward'. Another pattern of bit becoming increasingly popular with some trainers is called the Dexter ring bit, a type originally used for harness horses. It is often used on horses who might otherwise tend to 'hold on' to one side of a bit, and thus be harder to keep straight, and/or those who would otherwise be rather 'strong'. This rather weird-looking device has a ring that fits in the horse's mouth and round his lower jaw, and is attached to a snaffle-type mouthpiece. It seems to work well for most horses who wear it.

Headgear   Various forms of headgear may be applied to horses, the common intention being to try to maximize performance.

Blinkers   These are fitted over a horse's head with holes for the eyes and ears, with cowls fitted to cut out the horse's vision to the rear but allowing full forward vision. Blinkers have long been in use and were formerly closely associated in many minds with horses who didn't concentrate on racing or were reluctant to put their best hoof forward. It is true that they can assist the jockey of a horse who might otherwise run lazily or tend to stop once he hits the front, but it is also true that some horses who

This horse is wearing blinkers and a cross noseband.

race habitually in blinkers seem perfectly genuine performers in such gear and thus do not deserve to be stigmatized for wearing them. It is worth being cautious, however, of a horse racing in blinkers for the first time (which may be noted on some racecards), because there is usually a degree of trial and error about this – they are not fitted on a whim, but because something in the horse's past performances suggests they might be worth trying. Sometimes, first-time blinkers have a positive effect, causing the horse to travel more freely (and thus making it easier for the jockey to maintain or vary his tactical position in a race) and perhaps run on more resolutely at the finish. However, the change to his field of vision can sometimes have a more dramatic effect than desired, causing the horse to run much too freely, to the detriment of his finishing position.

Modifications on blinkers are *eyeshields*, in which the eye cowls are covered by mesh or a transparent material, and *eyecovers*, in which one eye only is covered by an opaque material. These are pretty rare and usually applied if the horse has some kind of eye problem that the trainer feels requires protection from flying particles of the racing surface or, possibly, from flying insects.

Visor   A visor is similar to blinkers, the key difference being that (usually both) eye cowls have slits in them to allow a limited degree of side or rear vision. The idea behind this is to maintain the horse's concentration on going forward, whilst allowing some degree of visual reassurance of the proximity of other horses.

Cheekpieces   Usually made of sheepskin, these attach to the cheekpieces of the horse's bridle (the leather straps of the bridle that run down the sides of his head), making him look like a Victorian gentleman with full side whiskers. They work in a way broadly similar to blinkers, in that they modify his rear and sideways vision, thus helping him to concentrate. There is a view that they may also have a pacifying effect during the racing preliminaries.

Hood   Like blinkers, a hood fits over the horse's head, but it has eyeholes with no cowls (to allow full vision) and padded ear covers, into which the ears fit snugly, making the horse look like a member of some dodgy extremist cult. All horses have acute hearing, but some become hypersensitive to noise in exciting environments, and a hood will often have a calming effect on such a horse at a big, bustling meeting. It is worth noting how a hooded horse reacts to such challenges as parading past a brass band going full blast in front of the grandstand but, generally speaking, when applied, hoods seem beneficial. A hood can, in principle, be fitted in conjunction with blinkers.

Earplugs   Not surprisingly, these are sometimes applied to horses hypersensitive to noise and, where used, seem to have a beneficial effect. Once a horse has been fitted with earplugs, it is not permitted for the jockey to remove them during the course of a race.

Tongue tie/strap   As mentioned in Chapter 5, a tongue tie may indicate that there has previously been some concern about a horse's breathing during a race, in which malpositioning of his tongue can be a factor. A tongue tie, which fits over the tongue and fastens beneath the jaw (but might not be obvious to a casual glance), may help prevent this. If there is evidence from past form that this device seems effective for the individual wearing it, its presence should not be a cause for concern.

Declaration of Equipment

If a horse is to race in blinkers, eyeshields or eyecovers, a visor, cheekpieces, hood or tongue tie, these items must be declared as part of his intended equipment at the time that he is declared a runner. There are various constraints and penalties in place in cases of changes or omissions.

Bandages and boots   In the past, it was not uncommon to see racehorses wearing leg bandages, often applied to support tendons. Such bandages are a lot rarer nowadays, probably because of advances in the treatment of tendon injuries. Also, trainers generally try to avoid fitting bandages to racehorses whenever they can, because of the potential dangers of them becoming loose. However, they will be applied if this is considered necessary. Occasionally, a horse may be bandaged to protect a relatively minor injury, such as a cut that doesn't interfere with his ability to race, from dirt or mud. There is a convention in horse care that, if one leg is bandaged, the opposite one should be also (so if one foreleg is bandaged, then the other foreleg is too) to avoid the undamaged leg being overloaded, so it is rare to see a horse of any type with a bandage on just

The closing stages of a race. The leading horse is wearing boots; a fairly rare sight nowadays.

one leg. Boots are widely used in other equestrian disciplines as a protective measure but, unless fitted correctly, have the potential to cause rub injuries (either of themselves or because dirt or mud have got underneath them), and the additional weight added to the legs is a particular factor in racing. However, as with bandages, they may occasionally be fitted to racehorses if connections feel that their protective role outweighs the potential disadvantages.

Owners' Colours

The most obvious visual aids to identifying the runners are, of course, the owners' colours worn by jockeys, which will be shown against each horse on the racecard. However, it's worth noting that sometimes an owner will run two horses (or even more) in the same race, in which case they will carry what are fundamentally the same colours, but with an identifying tweak (commonly, a different colour/design on the cap). In such cases, it is necessary to note which variation applies to which horse. Another form of identification that might seem worth noting is the number on the cloth beneath the saddle, which is the horse's racecard number (not his draw number). Seen in close-up, as the horses are walking around the paddock, it is easy to think that this would be very useful. However, in practice, you need to be careful with this because, although it *may* be useful, there

A head-on shot of the field taking a hurdle. Note that three of the jockeys have fairly similar colours, incorporating mauve, two of their horses are wearing headgear (blinkers and hood), and all three of their mounts have breastgirths; an illustration of why you may need to take care to ensure that you follow 'your' horse in a race.

is a chance of confusion if the cloth starts flapping in the race itself and/or is partially obscured. In such circumstances, you may think, for example, that you are watching horse number three, when you are actually watching number thirteen.

GOING TO THE START

Watching horses going to the start should be an easy short step if you have just been looking at them in the paddock.

Some major races have a pre-race parade, during which the contestants (initially led by handlers) parade in front of the grandstand in racecard order in walk, before being released to canter down to the start. I'm not personally a fan of these – my sympathies are with the jockeys, who just want to get their charges safely and calmly to the start, and to get on with the race – but they do give spectators a final chance to see how the horses have handled the preliminaries. Generally, however, once the horses leave the paddock, they go straight out onto the course and canter to the start.

In most races on most courses, the start is not particularly near the winning post (which is located opposite the stands and thus near the paddock exit), so the jockeys' aim is to canter their horses steadily from the racecourse entrance to the start, either on the course itself or along an all-weather strip to the side. This allows the horses to have a further warm-up before the race itself. (In cases where the start of the race is near the entrance to the course, jockeys commonly canter a furlong or two down the

Runners getting into line to parade before a big race.

About to set off to the start.

Preparing to canter to the start at Ascot. This horse is wearing a breastgirth and cheekpieces. Note the covering of grass on the track.

Cantering to the start on an all-weather strip.

course before returning to the start.) What a jockey wants to feel, whilst cantering to the start, is the horse moving fluently and enthusiastically without flinging his head about or trying to rush – and that is the ideal picture for race-goers. Sometimes, however, this doesn't happen.

As mentioned in the context of watching horses in the paddock, some tend to get 'het up' before a race and will have a natural instinct, once they reach the track, to go too hard and expend too much energy – even, in extreme cases, to try to **bolt**. The connections of such a horse may therefore seek permission for him to be taken down early, before the others have left the paddock, on the basis that others going down at the same time may 'light him up'. A jockey taking a horse down early will try to keep him very steady, riding at a slow canter or sometimes even keeping to a trot. If a cantering horse is threatening to get very strong, it is not unusual for the jockey to turn him somewhat sideways (typically with the horse's head over the running rail) because this positioning 'breaks the horse's stride', making it physically harder for him to launch into a gallop. So long as a horse who is taken down early remains under a reasonable level of control, this should not prejudice his chances in the race itself.

The opposite of this scenario is a reluctance to go down – i.e. the horse shows a disinclination to canter to the start. This may be indicated by him backing up, trying to whip round in the opposite direction, bucking and plunging or, in some cases, 'planting'

Sometimes, a horse will develop the quirk of behaving very strangely when leaving the paddock and going onto the course. The horse in these photos was a case in point, although he was fine in the actual race. One method tried as a means of persuading him was having a pony accompany him. Here, once he is out on the course, his jockey hurries to mount and send him on his way. In the USA, it is common practice for a mounted racehorse to be actually led to the start from a second rider on another mount – a practice known as 'ponying'.

– simply refusing to move. The precise reasons for this may be complex, but in simple terms they may be as follows:

1. The horse has fallen out of love with racing, and doesn't really want to know. Even if such a horse is persuaded to the start, his attitude may be further evidenced by a reluctance to start on terms with the others, or to exert himself greatly in the race itself. Although this does happen on occasion, such horses are a relatively rare sight because (a) keeping them in training is a waste of the owner's money and (b) if they develop a habit of not going into the starting stalls (on the flat) or failing to 'jump off' (under NH rules) they will be officially banned.
2. The horse has an exaggeratedly strong herd instinct and is reluctant to move away from an area where he senses other horses in the proximity (still in the paddock, in the nearby stables, horsebox park, etc.). Alternatively, he may just be a nervous type who has developed a kind of horsy 'stage fright'. Either of these types may be perfectly okay if another runner 'gives them a lead' (comes beside them and then canters off just in front of them). Again, once such horses have arrived at the start, their prospects in the race itself should be undiminished.

A sight still rare on UK racecourse is that of a horse being 'ponyed' to the start. This procedure, which is standard practice in the USA, consists of the mounted runners being escorted (in fact, led) from the paddock to the start by a second rider (not a participant in the race) on another horse. (The term 'pony' is used because many of these escort animals are, in fact, ponies, but size is not an issue, whereas suitability for the job is.) The practice seems to have been introduced to the UK by American connections whose horses were qualified to take part in major races, and who received permission from the UK authorities to have them escorted to the start in the manner that would have been usual for them. It has not become standard practice in the UK, but, now it is permitted, it is employed on rare occasions to help get a particularly tricky horse to the start. If the intention is to use this method, this must be notified at the time the horse is declared a runner, and both the pony himself and the manner in which he is used for the job are subject to a number of regulations. The horse being led in this way has to go to the start steadily before the other runners, so as not to delay the race.

AT THE START

Watching horses and jockeys down at the start is a very interesting aspect of race-going and it is well worth going to the start of a race or two at any course that allows this. Apart from anything else, it can be worth a trip to the start just to hear the banter between jockeys – although this may prove educational for those from a sheltered background. Some courses offer a guided minibus service to get to distant starts.

As the horses approach the start, the jockeys will ease them down so that, typically, they will travel the last few yards in trot or walk. If a horse arrives at the start still travelling quite fast, he is likely to have been exerting himself more than the jockey would have wished all the way down. It is worth noting, at this point, whether any horses have become particularly hot and sweaty and, if so, to what extent this relates to the weather conditions. On a hot, humid summer's day, it is to be expected that most

Unlike in showjumping, racehorses in the UK don't have a 'practice jump' before NH races, so jockeys often let them have a view of a fence to remind them what's about to happen. Having been shown the first fence, these runners are now about to turn back towards the start.

At many courses nowadays, the assembly point prior to the start is in a chute off the main track, and there are usually sections of a hurdle and a fence adjacent to this point at which jockeys can also 'show the horse the fence'.

horses will be a little damp if they have just cantered half a mile or so, but it is not a good sign if one is awash with sweat, nor is it if a horse is significantly sweaty on a cool or chilly day.

The horses' demeanour is also of interest. A horse walking calmly around **on a long rein** with the jockey's legs in a normal racing position is a sign that the horse is taking proceedings in his stride. However, if a jockey has taken his feet out of the stirrups and has his legs hanging down long, this may illustrate something a bit different. Horses can learn to pick up on all kinds of signals from the rider on top and some very much associate the jockey's 'short leg position, good hold of reins' with being the 'go' signal, whereas the 'relaxed, long legs, long rein' posture is associated with what happens after work at home, during the warming down phase on the way back to the stables. Therefore, if a jockey feels that the horse is getting a bit wound up on the way to the start, once there he may adopt this latter posture as an aid to keeping the horse 'under wraps'. This is the sort of horsemanship that serves riders well in all forms of equitation, and can often prove successful in racing.

In addition to the horses and jockeys, there will be various people at, or in reach of, the start, to help the process go smoothly.

If a horse is known to become a bit excited or anxious before the start, the presence of a handler with whom he is familiar may help to keep him calm. Such a person may assist in various ways, such as having a cloth to hand to wipe of any excessive sweat. (It can be particularly useful to wipe sweat off a horse's neck, because sweaty reins don't make a jockey's job any easier.) For jump racing, where there are no starting stalls, a

Horses relaxing after working at home. The riders have long reins and their feet out of the stirrups, a posture sometimes adopted to encourage horses to relax before the start of a race.

Adjusting equipment at the start.

Runners assembling behind the stalls before a flat race.

A big field preparing to line up for the start of a steeplechase.

handler may get permission to lead a horse into the barrier to make sure he jumps off on terms with the rest of the field. This ploy is sometimes used for horses who have become reluctant to start and for those who, as a result of 'stage fright', have developed a tendency to react to the start with a kind of 'rabbit in the headlights' response.

The starter's assistant's key roles are to check that all the runners are down at the start and, on the flat, to remind jockeys of their draw number. Another important role is to assist jockeys in last-minute checks to their equipment, in particular to ensure that girths are sufficiently tight – a check that is very often followed by timely adjustment.

A farrier and vet will usually be on hand at the start of a race (or readily available) to deal with issues such as a last-minute reshoeing and checking the horse's subsequent soundness, or, in the vet's case, attending to any last-minute concerns about a horse's welfare, whether raised by the jockey or brought about by an inadvertent kick from another runner, or a horse having a problem whilst in the stalls.

For flat races, stalls handlers will be in attendance at the start, occasionally accompanied by a horse behavioural specialist if one of the runners has exhibited particular problems in the past. The handlers work under instructions from the starter, and it is fascinating to see the various ploys and equipment they use to persuade horses into the stalls as quickly and efficiently as possible – although sometimes patience can be a key factor. The task of handlers is potentially quite dangerous and their willingness to climb into limited spaces in the stalls to help pacify a fractious horse is quite remarkable. (Perhaps oddly, a horse's difficult behaviour in entering the stalls, or whilst in them, is not necessarily a guide to how he will perform in the actual race.)

The starter is in overall charge of what takes place in the lead-up to the start, and of the actual start itself, and has the responsibility of ensuring that all regulations and practices relating to starting a race are adhered to. In carrying out these responsibilities he has powers to, for instance, report recalcitrant jockeys to the stewards and to stipulate a horse's withdrawal from the race for either medical or behavioural reasons. It is, of course, a key part of his role to try to ensure that all the runners are given as even a chance as possible when the race starts, and this can require having eyes like a hawk (and a spare set in the back of his head) to ensure, for instance, that the stalls in a flat race don't open at a time when one runner is, perhaps, rearing, or that the barrier in a jumps race doesn't release at a moment when a horse is standing sideways on, or has even turned round. If, when down at the start, you watch and listen to the starter, you are likely to witness an interesting blend of diplomat and martinet in action.

Once the horses are under way, provided that the starter doesn't wave his flag to signify a false start, the flag man, situated some distance down the course (but before the first obstacle in a jumping race) will saunter serenely away from his position on the course and duck under the rails out of harm's way. If, however, the starter signals a false start, the flag man will have to stand his ground and wave his own flag vigorously. This is not a role for the faint-hearted or, indeed, for the infirm.

Leaving the stalls at the start of a flat race.

Preparing to line up for the start of a steeplechase – and they're off!

WATCHING HORSES TAKE A JUMP

Watching a field of horses fly over a jump (ideally, a steeplechase fence, but also a flight of hurdles) is major thrill for all fans of NH racing. If you have gone down to the start of the race, you won't have time to see the field over the first fence, but you will easily be able to stroll down to it (or back to the one before the start) to see the runners jump it on the next circuit. If you've just been in or around the paddock, you will be quite near the fences in the finishing straight so, again, you can easily get close to one of them.

One of the things that often surprises newcomers to racing is the noise level associated with a field of horses jumping. There is the increasing sound of drumming hooves as they approach, the voices of jockeys calling for room (not always politely) and verbally encouraging their mounts, the thud of hooves against the take-off rail of a fence if a horse **gets in close** and the brushing sound as most of the field flick through the forgiving upper inches of the fence. In a big field of hurdlers, if several rap the upper rail of the obstacle, as is often the case, the noise can almost resemble repeated gunfire.

Jumping a hurdle.

Soaring over a steeplechase fence.

Another thing that can come as a surprise is the distance at which horses take off from the obstacles. This, in fact, can be particularly surprising for newcomers to racing who are, themselves, riders competing in disciplines such as showjumping, where the usual approach to a fence will be from a steady canter, and the aim will be to reach a fairly precise take-off point. A bold steeplechaser, taking off level with the wings of a fence and flying out to land well beyond it is a sight to behold.

If you intend to watch the horses over a jump, there are some points to consider in respect of your own, and others', safety. To deal with the latter first, don't even think about trying to take a picture using flash photography, which could potentially unsight runners or riders. Secondly, don't even think about erecting an umbrella as the runners approach the fence and, preferably, don't stand near a fence with one erected. Although it's perhaps being cautious to mention this, I would also advise against viewing runners nearing a fence through binoculars on a sunny day, in case these reflect the glare.

From a personal viewpoint, although the fences in the finishing straight of most courses will be well railed off from spectators, this is not necessarily the case with those out '**in the country**', particularly at some smaller courses (and most point-to-point courses). Therefore, if you go to stand close to a fence, don't stand too close, and remain vigilant. Bear in mind that, very occasionally, a horse may try to run out on the approach to a fence and, if a horse falls and gets loose, he will not necessarily stick to the track when he gets to his feet. Therefore, at or near fences, enjoy the spectacle, but keep vigilant.

An early stage in a point-to-point. Here, the riderless horse seems happy to accompany the other runners but, when spectating at close quarters, you should always watch out for loose horses. (Photo: Ginni Beard)

Finally, in the interests of all concerned, you should be aware that nowadays, all races at professional tracks are followed by a vehicle filming the race to provide evidence if anything happens that the stewards believe requires investigation, and also by an ambulance. These vehicles typically drive along tracks to the inside of the course, so it is necessary to keep an eye out for them whilst the race is in progress.

WATCHING THE RACE UNFOLD

Your view of the race overall will depend largely on your chosen vantage point. The geography of some courses is such that, with binoculars, you can get a pretty good view of the whole thing from a particular point. At other courses, the best overview will be from some part of the elevated stands. Many courses also show the race on a big screen in the grandstand area and, if you happen to be in that area at the start of the race, this offers the advantage of a close-up view. The screen may also show a post-race rerun so, if you've been somewhere out on the course during the live action and want to check a point of detail this can provide the opportunity to do so.

Although going to the start, or watching the action at a fence, are very interesting

This view from the stands at Cheltenham shows spectators taking up various vantage points. Note also the big screen out on the course.

aspects of racing, for a race in which you've had a bet, you may prefer to concentrate on watching events unfold as closely as possible. The slight irony here is that, in focusing on the horse you've backed, you may get only a limited overview of the whole thing. However, not focusing primarily on 'your' horse would be almost inhuman, so how is it best done?

This will, to a considerable extent, depend on the type of race, and particularly on the number of runners and the distance. Since the fundamentally important point is being able to identify your horse, you will need to have used the racecard to identify the jockey's colours and, as stated earlier in the section on the paddock, it is useful to note other factors such as the horse's colour, any particular markings and any equipment that may help to identify him. Then, on the flat and particularly in a big-field sprint, it is important to note the horse's stall number, so you can focus on this as the field leaves the stalls. When this happens, the field may either bunch together (in which case individuals will be obscured) or split into two or more groups (in which case you need to identify which group your horse has joined). Similarly, over jumps – particularly in big-field hurdles, the early stages can be a bit of a blur, so it's useful to identify your horse as soon as possible. In smaller fields and/or in longer races, it is easier to follow proceedings and, in such races, to keep an eye on what the other runners (perhaps an opponent you fear) are doing.

Although the grey horse in the centre is sweating, the three runners in this photo still seem to be travelling well at present – the jockeys are sitting motionless.

When focusing on your horse you will, ideally, want to see him travelling smoothly, without appearing to fight his jockey, and without needing to be chased along. The jockey sitting virtually motionless during the early and middle stages of the race is generally a good sign, pretty much regardless of where the horse is positioned in the field, because it usually suggests that he is fairly happy with how the horse is travelling. However, it is also important to realize that most horses, regardless of the distance over which they run, will have an ideal 'cruising speed' and being asked to go significantly faster than this for any length of time will materially reduce their overall effectiveness and, in NH races, increase the likelihood that they may make jumping errors. Thus sometimes, if a jockey feels that his horse is almost 'flat to the boards' in the mid-part of a race, he will not ask for more effort at that stage but will sit still and hope that the horse will run on in the closing stages, hopefully staying on past opponents who may have gone too fast too early.

It is usually in the latter stages that a race 'unfolds', as the riders ask their mounts for efforts that they hope will get them involved in the finish. At this stage, unless his horse is travelling clearly better than the opposition, a jockey will become more animated, sitting lower in the saddle and beginning to kick with his legs and drive forward with his hands and upper body in rhythm with his horse's strides.

Nearing the finish of a flat race – a clear leader but a battle for the places. A lot can change in the final moments of a race.

One exception to this, sometimes seen in an experienced jockey who is well-attuned to his mount, is when a jockey is trying to 'nurse' his horse home. Typically, this may happen on soft ground in staying races, when the horse in question is an honest type who will keep trying his best with minimum urging, but is starting to 'run on empty'. To an onlooker, such a horse may still seem to be going well, but the jockey will realize that there is 'nothing left in the tank'. Getting physically vigorous with such a horse (let alone hitting him) will be very unlikely to produce any extra effort, and will be more likely to unbalance him, so the jockey's best chance of winning or obtaining the best position is to maintain his own balance and avoid panicking. Of course, when a jockey gets beaten in such circumstances, there is bound to be some criticism, but this will mainly come from people who are far more familiar with lying on sofas than riding tired racehorses.

If it is evident, before the closing stages, that your horse is out of contention, it makes sense to switch your attention to those who are fighting out the finish, because you may see a performance worth noting for a later date. In addition to the manner in which the race is run, there may be a horse finishing particularly well after being trapped **in a pocket** or outpaced, who might merit consideration next time he runs (in the latter case, perhaps over a longer distance).

The closing stages of a hurdle race. The jockeys fighting out the finish are currently just swinging their whips.

Use of the Whip

One point I should perhaps touch upon here is the use of the whip, which I realize can be a misunderstood and contentious topic. One way (albeit perhaps a rather crude one) of expressing the misunderstanding is that jockeys hit horses repeatedly without constraint to make them go faster. In fact, the main method of asking a horse to increase or sustain his effort is for the jockey to drive with his upper body and kick or squeeze (depending on individual style) with his legs. The effectiveness of these actions may be enhanced by prudent and timely use of a whip, but only if this is done at the precise moment in the horse's stride pattern when the horse can respond, and not if it is done in a manner likely to unbalance the horse, or with a force that would make him tense up in response.

Historically, it is true that there were types of whip used in racing that could poten-tially hurt a horse and various cases of abuse that, in addition to being unpalatable, were probably counterproductive as often as not – as suggested above, repeatedly hitting a tiring horse hard would be more likely to unbalance him or cause him to 'curl up' in defence than to assist his progress. In times past, stewards had the power to penalize a jockey for abuse of the whip, but this was done largely on the basis of individual judge-ment. However, there were, for many years, individuals involved in racing (including some jockeys) who pressed for changes in the rules relating to use of the whip, and this resulted in incremental modifications to the type of whip permitted and the manner of its use. Nowadays, the BHA (which consults with major animal charities and veterinary advisers) has strict rules about the length and construction of whips permitted in racing (which are of an energy-absorbing design) and also about the number of times and the manner in which the whip can be used in a race,* and for what purpose, with jockeys who transgress these rules being punished by suspensions (which can be severe, if offences are cumulative) and monetary fines. The Professional Jockeys Association provides guidance to members based on the BHA rules, and correct handing of the whip is taught in the racing schools. My view, for what it's worth, is that the current rules strike a pretty good balance between moderate use of the whip for the legitimate purposes of keeping horses focused, straight and putting their best hoof forward, without compromising their welfare.

THE AFTERMATH

Immediately Post-race

Once a race is over, there is still much of interest to see. It can be heart-warming to witness the level of involvement of the stable staff and the degree of sportsmanship

Runners easing down at the end of a race.

---

* Sometimes, once a jockey has 'picked up' (started to use the whip), he will continue to swing it in rhythm with his driving upper body, only actually applying it on a few occasions. People unfamiliar with this scenario may misinterpret it as constant application of the whip, but this will not be the case, as will be evident either from a head-on view or from a more informed analysis of the jockey's action

Delighted stable staff leading in the winner of the Queen Anne Stakes, Royal Ascot.

that is often evident between jockeys, owners and trainers. As the horses pull up after the finish, it is common to see beaten jockeys congratulate the winning rider, particularly if it is a major success for a younger rider, or one coming back from injury. If you consider that the jockey on the second horse will have been doing his damnedest throughout the race, perhaps to be deprived of several thousand pounds by a rapidly diminishing neck, it will be evident that this reaction is unlikely to be fake.

The joy on the face of the stable hand who comes out to meet the winner and lead him in is also something worth seeing. It is the stable staff who form the closest relationships with the horses, spending hours each day in their care, helping to nurse them if they are sick or injured, and developing what is almost a proprietorial attitude towards them. When interviewed post-race, these people are frequently so overcome with emotion that they struggle to articulate their feelings – but they can be guaranteed to get on with the business of ensuring that their charge is cooled down and made comfortable after his exertions.

To revert to financial considerations, it is notable that trainers and owners of beaten horses can often be seen to congratulate winning connections, despite the fact that losing a major race can have very considerable implications. On the flat, in particular, being narrowly beaten in one of the Classic races not only makes a big difference in

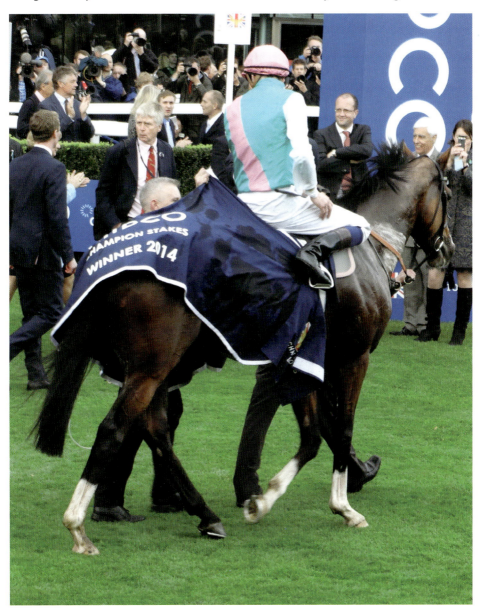

Returning to the winner's enclosure.

terms of prize money – it may also impact on a horse's future stud value that could, over his lifetime, add up to millions of pounds. Over jumps, a trainer who has been handling a horse for the best part of a decade, and has spent the whole season priming his charge for the really big day, may find it hard to swallow if he loses out in the Cheltenham Gold Cup or the Grand National by half a length. Shaking hands with the winner's trainer must, in such circumstances, be a test of character, but it is by no means a rare sight.

Winner's and Unsaddling Enclosures

When the runners are led in after the race, they will go to be unsaddled. The winner will usually go to a dedicated winner's enclosure and there will be adjacent berths for the placed horses, while the other runners are attended to close by. While the horses are unsaddled and offered a drink, there will be discussions between the jockeys and the horses' connections, which can be quite revealing. The cynical might assume that all the jockeys except the winning rider will be trotting out excuses but, while there may be an element of this, generally speaking trainers will value jockeys' feedback, which may inform future plans for their horses. It should be remembered that only one horse can win a race, and it is unlikely that all the other jockeys made mistakes!

On the way to the winner's enclosure a jockey gives his post-race opinion to the press.

A popular winner almost immersed in the crowd.

Weighing in, Objections, and Stewards' Enquiries

After the race, the jockeys of the winner and the placed horses must weigh in, to confirm that they have been riding at the allotted weight.

It is only after the 'weighed in' announcement has been given that the result is official, and most bookmakers wait to hear this before paying out winning bets. The other occasion when this will be delayed is if there is an objection and/or stewards' enquiry that could, again, affect the result.

Objections can be raised by the jockey, owner or trainer of a horse if any one of them considers that the jockey of the provisional winner or other placed horse has done or allowed something to interfere with their own horse's chances of winning or being placed. (It is usual for a jockey who wishes to object to check this with the owner/trainer

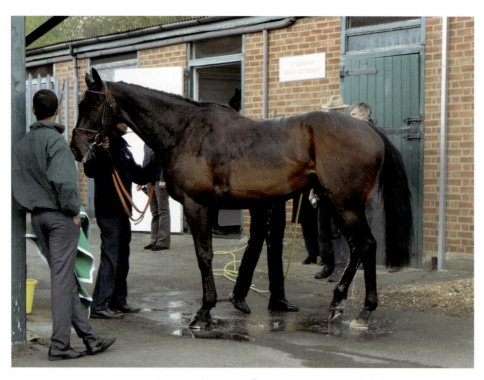

Attention is given to the post-race comfort of the runners. Here, the horse is thoroughly washed down, then walked to begin the drying-off process (note the blue earplugs).

before the objection is lodged. There is a fee for lodging an objection, which will be returned if it is upheld, but forfeited if the stewards consider it frivolous or spurious.) Typical reasons for lodging an objection would include barging through a gap that wasn't really there, thus colliding with and impeding the victim, or one horse 'taking another's ground' (hanging/drifting into or across him) in the closing stages (or, in jump racing, at the final fence/hurdle, thus hampering the affected horse). Objections of any kind must be lodged before the 'weighed in' announcement, and will be announced over the public address system.

Once an official objection is lodged, the stewards are obliged to investigate. They may also have their own concerns about the incident, in which case the racecourse announcer will declare both an objection and a stewards' enquiry. At other times, the stewards may declare their own enquiry, without an objection having been raised. This may be because, for some reason, a horse's connections didn't wish to object to some incident they considered unworthy of raising, or it may be that the stewards have noticed some incident earlier in the race that they decided to look into. In the latter case, the racecourse announcer will report the nature of the enquiry and, where relevant (for instance, if there was a mid-race collision between horses not involved in the finish), state that it does not affect the initial winner or the placed horses. Clearly, if an objection/enquiry does concern the winner and/or placed horses, the result is not official until the stewards have completed their deliberations, so bookies won't pay out prior to this.

CHAPTER 8

Racing Terminology

Racing is a sport absolutely riddled with idiomatic terms – some archaic, others quite modern – that are used habitually by racing presenters, commentators and the compilers of racecards and form guides. This chapter is essentially a glossary of such terms and I have, where necessary, used it to provide a fuller explanation of what the terms may signify in different situations.

For ease of access, the terms are listed alphabetically. Within each entry, any reference to another entry is set in bold. Within the main text of the book, terms listed within this section are set in bold at their first use.

Action   The way a horse moves in his faster gaits. This is closely related to his **conformation** – *see* that entry for further details.

All out   A horse who has made maximum effort to attain/retain his finishing position.

Bar   Bookies' shorthand for 'the rest of the horses'. Sometimes, a bookmaker's list of odds for a race (or a betting forecast), won't show the actual price for every horse at longer odds, but ends with a phrase such as '20–1 bar'. This doesn't mean that all the unquoted horses are priced at 20–1; some may be at much longer odds. This rather old phrase is sometimes replaced nowadays by the more explanatory 'upwards others'.

Bolt/Bolted up   Horses do, on occasion, 'bolt', which means to take total charge of their rider and career off in unstoppable fashion. This is usually a reaction to a flood of adrenalin, caused by total over-excitement or as a panic response. However, the term 'bolted up' has a very different meaning – it is commonly used figuratively to mean that a horse won a race very easily, by a significant margin. (*See also* **running away**.)

Changing his legs   When a horse gallops (or canters) he will lead the sequence of his strides consistently with either his left or right foreleg. If a horse begins to 'change his legs' (i.e. the leading leg) this usually indicates that he is getting tired, unbalanced and/or **feeling the ground** in some combination. Most commonly, it happens in the closing stages of a race, when the primary factor is tiredness; if it happens at an earlier stage it may well indicate a more significant physical problem. (*See also* **lost his action**.)

Clear   Means that the horse referred to has a significant lead over the rest of the runners. 'Going clear' suggests that he is still increasing his lead; 'remains clear' means that an established lead is unaltered. A commentator may further refine the information by estimating how far the horse is ahead in terms of **lengths**.

Codes   This is a convenient word often used as 'shorthand' in conversations that refer to flat racing and jump racing – i.e. these are the two 'codes' of racing. Although, nowadays, there is a great deal of common ground between the rules for these types of racing, there are still distinctions that relate to the inherent differences between them. However, although the term 'codes' may be used in a detailed discussion about a specific point, it is commonly used in a more casual context – for example, it might be said of a horse who combines flat racing and hurdling that he is 'an effective performer under both codes'.

Conformation   This describes a horse's physical make-up. Thoroughbred racehorses, although all of the same breed, vary considerably in this respect and an individual horse's conformation will have a material effect on how he handles different conditions. Some internal aspects of this will be unclear on simple observation – for example, a horse with a particularly powerful heart and lungs (the capacities of which do vary between individuals) may be at an advantage when there are demands on sheer stamina (e.g. heavy going; long distances) but, since horses are not transparent, this may be evident only by reference to his past racing record.

   The features of conformation that will be most visible to an observer with a reasonably keen eye – and perhaps most informative – are the angle of slope of the shoulders and the way in which the limbs operate when the horse is moving at canter and gallop (so watching horses canter to the start can be very informative). Generally speaking, and put simply, a horse whose shoulders slope at around 45 degrees, and whose legs seem to swing out freely forward, are referred to as having a 'low action' (an older term is 'daisy-cutting') and tend to have relatively long strides. Such horses tend to 'skim' over the ground and are often most effective on a fairly sound (e.g. good, or good to firm) surface. However, one consequence of this action is that each footfall is in contact with the ground for a relatively long time, and this can count against such horses on holding/ heavy ground, when they may tend to get 'stuck in the mud'. More or less the converse may apply to horses with more upright shoulders, and whose limbs move in a more 'up and down' manner, a bit like pistons. This limb movement produces more concussion and such horses may not be very comfortable on firmer surfaces. However, in addition to perhaps being more comfortable on softer ground, the 'up and down' action of their limbs can help them get through it more effectively than their low-actioned rivals. (It should be stressed that, while observation of movement can provide a useful guide, horses exist mainly to make fools of people, and there are individuals out there whose racing records defy physical analysis. There is an old saying that 'a good horse goes on any ground' – this is not actually true, because there are, and have been, horses demonstrably top-class but only when conditions suit. However, it is generally the case that horses with good all-round conformation are likely to be effective across a fairly wide range of conditions.)

Connections (of a horse)   This term is used casually to apply to the owner(s) and trainer of a horse – those most likely to be involved in making decisions about race entries, welfare, etc.

Cover   To have cover means that a horse is tucked in behind others in the race, and thus is usually racing in a fairly relaxed way. Jockeys on horses who tend to be **keen** will try to get cover in the earlier stages of a race for that reason. (*See also* **seeing too**

much daylight.) Jockeys may also try to get cover in the slipstream of runners in front of them if racing into a strong headwind. (The term 'covering' is also used to describe a stallion mating with a mare.)

Delivered late   Said when a jockey does his best to put his horse in front shortly before the finishing line. This is not (usually) motivated by the jockey's desire to show off, but because some horses 'down tools' once they realize they are in the lead (*see* **idling**) and, if this happens any distance from the finish it is very hard to re-galvanize them if there is a late challenge from another runner. There are various psychological theories as to why some horses are like this, one being that they have a strong herd instinct and are not natural 'leaders'. Some weight is given to this theory by the opposite scenario, which is that other horses seem to enjoy going further clear of their rivals once they take the lead, with minimal encouragement from the saddle. This is further evidence that different horses have very different characters. (*See also* **hold-up horse**.)

Drawn/posted wide   Drawn wide refers to a flat race, generally one on a turning track, where a horse's starting stall (draw) is to the outside and is therefore a potential or actual disadvantage. In the early stages of a race, a commentator may refer to a runner being posted wide if, as a result of his draw, the jockey has not been able to manoeuvre towards a position more towards the inside. If this situation persists, the term **trapped wide** may be used.

Dropped his hands   Said of a jockey who has, in effect, stopped riding in the closing stages of a race. When a jockey is riding a horse actively, one of his actions will be to push forward with his hands, arms and upper body, in rhythm with the horse's strides. When a horse is being eased down (e.g. once a race has finished) the jockey will stop riding actively, become more upright in his body and, usually, lower his hands onto the base of the horse's neck, which the horse will take as a signal that he can ease down. Sometimes, a jockey may perform a (usually modified) version of this action before the winning post is reached. One reason for doing this (particularly relevant to handicaps) is that the jockey may not want to win by too wide a margin, since this may attract the attention of the official handicapper, who may then increase the horse's rating significantly, thus affecting his prospects in future races. Another reason is to avoid giving a horse an unnecessarily hard race – if the horse has another engagement in the near future or, despite winning the current one, is clearly getting very tired, there is no point in doing more than necessary. However, there are inherent dangers in this practice: some horses, if their rider drops his hands, may slow down more quickly, and to a greater extent, than the rider anticipated and there are, from time to time, cases where a jockey actually throws away a race by doing this. It should be said that these are highly unlikely to be cynical instances of corrupt practice because to do this intentionally at the business end of a race, in front of a crowded grandstand, the judge and the official stewards, would be like standing over a bleeding corpse, waving a dagger, in front of a police cordon. However, when it happens, it brings down upon the jockey the wrath of racing officialdom, the horse's connections, and all the punters who would otherwise have been collecting their winnings – and is likely to incur significant penalties in the shape of fines and suspension. Sometimes, when a jockey drops his hands and *nearly* gets caught out but manages to hold on and win, the stewards may have a warning word in his ear – and there are occasions when a jockey who has held on by a diminish-ing margin will clearly look relieved (and a bit sheepish) on the way to the unsaddling enclosure. Easing down when winning a race is perfectly legitimate – sometimes desir-able – but needs to be done with considerable discretion.

There are two rather more bizarre – but not unknown – reasons why a jockey may drop his hands. One concerns unfamiliarity with crucial course markers and the other may be some mixture of this and simple inattention. In respect of the former, some courses have, shortly before the winning post, another post of some sort (perhaps a half-furlong marker) that might possibly be mistaken for the winning post by a jockey who is hard at work, and perhaps has his vision obscured by other runners. Occasion-ally – odd though it may seem – a course may have two winning posts, used for differ-ent races, again quite close. This arrangement seems a pretty bad idea and raises the question of why, if this is necessary, the posts cannot be collapsible/removable to avoid this potential problem – but it is not unknown and has the potential to cause genu-ine confusion. The other issue concerns long-distance jumping races around relatively small tracks that may, for instance, involve passing the winning post a total of three times during the race. It is not unknown for a jockey to 'lose count' during the course of such a race, make his 'winning run' a circuit early and stop riding in triumph, before the dreadful truth dawns. Since it is, in these circumstances, very difficult indeed to stoke up the horse and rejoin the race with any realistic chance of redemption, this tends to invite wrath from many quarters.

Dwells   Said of a horse who doesn't start promptly once the stalls open (flat race) or barrier is released (NH race). This may be the result of momentary inattention or inex-perience. (*See also* **run green**.) A horse who dwells will usually set off once he realizes what is required so, although not desirable, the delay may be fairly momentary. This is different from a horse who **plants**.

Evens (even money)   A bet where the win will pay the same as the stake: if you put £5 on an even money winner, you will get back £10 (the £5 win plus your original £5 stake).

False ground   A patch of the track where the surface is compromised in some way such that it may disrupt horses' stride patterns – e.g. slippery, boggy. Racecourse authorities try hard to ensure that there is no false ground at the track and, if a signifi-cant area becomes evident during a race meeting, this may, in severe cases, lead to abandonment of the rest of the meeting.

Favourite   The horse who is at the shortest odds at the start of the race. If more than one horse is at the same (shortest) odds, these horses are called joint favourites or co-favourites. The second favourite will be the horse with the second shortest odds.

Feeling the ground   This means that a horse is uncomfortable on the existing going, and usually relates to the fact that the ground is too firm for him. Physical reasons for this include the fact that the horse has (literally) thin soles to his feet – an issue for some Thoroughbreds – or that his **conformation** and natural **action** mean that he is feeling the effects of concussion on his limbs. A horse who is feeling the ground may be reluctant to gallop flat out at full stretch (sometimes termed **not letting himself**

down) and will thus have a rather high **head-carriage**, and he may also be prone to **changing his legs**.

Free to post   This means that the horse is going to the start very freely (quicker than the jockey would really like). In this context, 'to post' refers to the start – *see* **going to post**.

Gelded   A castrated male horse (gelding). Most male horses (in any branch of equitation) not intended for breeding are castrated, for reasons broadly similar to domestic dogs and cats being neutered. Horses who are not castrated are known as 'entire' and there are usually hopes that racehorses in this category may go on to become breeding stallions if their ancestry and racecourse successes advertise a potential role in that field.

Gets in close   Describes a horse taking off for a jump closer than ideal. This does not necessarily result in a major mistake, but will make the jump less fluent than ideal and will probably result in some loss of impetus in the first strides after landing.

Getting first run   This means that one of several horses on whom the jockey has ridden a **waiting race** has **gone for home** before the opposition. This may be a simple 'time to go' tactic on the jockey's part, or it may also involve his noticing that a rival is currently caught **in a pocket**.

Going   The prevailing condition of the ground. This can have a material effect on the chances of an individual horse – *see* **conformation**. Racecourse officials will always try to provide going that is safe to race on and broadly suitable for as wide a range of runners as possible but, despite their best efforts and improvements in watering and drainage systems, they are still, to some degree at the mercy of the elements. The current going at a course is always announced at least at the start of the day in which racing is due to take place (and conditions current at the time are often stated earlier than this). If, during the course of a day's racing, climatic influences cause the going to change, the revised description will be announced officially.

Going to post   An archaic phrase, which is still used by some commentators. Since most people equate 'the post' with the winning post, they may find it odd that this phrase actually refers to the start. It is perhaps more common nowadays to hear the phrase 'Going down [to the start]' although, for some races on some courses (such as Epsom) it would be strictly more accurate to say 'Going up …' (The term 'at the post' is sometimes used in a similar context, to mean 'at the start', but it is necessary to distinguish this from any time when the commentator may say, at the finish of a race: 'And, at the [winning] post it's ––– by a neck.')

Gone for home/goes on/sent on/takes it up   These are terms relating to a horse taking the lead. 'Gone for home' suggests that this is because the jockey has decided it's time to make a hopefully decisive move. 'Goes on' can mean the same thing, but might otherwise suggest that the horse has taken the lead because the previous leader has dropped back, rather than because his jockey has made a positive move to take over. 'Sent on' suggests that there has been a positive move by the jockey, perhaps at a fairly early stage because he thinks the existing pace is too slow, or as part of a move to make a break for the finish. 'Takes it up' simply means that the horse has gone to the lead, so can cover all the other scenarios.

Good traveller   A term applied to a horse who has a habit of galloping comfortably and in good balance in his races, looking as though he can readily quicken when asked to do so. Such a horse will always catch the eye, and may well go on to stamp his authority on the race with a smooth win. However, the term sometimes comes with a 'but' – 'He's a good traveller but doesn't always go through with it/finish off his races …' The easy assumption then is that the horse is irresolute, which could be true. However, there might be other factors involved. One possibility is that the horse is one-paced and, despite travelling easily at a certain speed, is unable to quicken in the closing stages of a race. Another is that the horse is naturally willing and/or competitive by nature, and will readily offer pretty much all he has to give from an early stage so that, towards the closing stages, he is 'running on empty'.

Hands and heels   The jockey is pushing the horse along with his body and legs, without recourse to the whip.

Hanging   A horse is said to be hanging when, instead of keeping to a straight line, he veers to some extent in a diagonal direction. (On a bend, a horse who hangs will veer off an evenly curved path, usually towards the outside of the bend.) There are several reasons why a horse may hang, the root cause being either temperamental or physical. Horses sometimes hang towards an object they find attractive, such as the exit back to the stables or box park, or towards one they perceive as a source of support (the running rail); in some circumstances they may hang away from the side on which the jockey is wielding the whip. They may also hang because they are trying to place less weight on a forelimb that is hurting them, or (on a bend) because they are being asked to turn in the direction that they find more difficult, such as a horse happier going left-handed being run on a tight right-handed track. When a horse is hanging there is always the chance that this may cause interference to other runners, so there is an obligation on the jockey to try to prevent this – although in some cases (especially if there is a significant physical issue), it may be far from easy. If a horse appears to be hanging away from the whip, the stewards will, as a minimum, expect the jockey to stop using it in the current hand, and perhaps to switch hands in an attempt to straighten the horse. Alternatively, the jockey may be expected to stop using the whip completely and employ both hands on the reins in an attempt to straighten the horse. Failure to take either course of action in these circumstances will usually result in the jockey being penalized.

Hard to train   This term is sometimes used to describe horses who make only occasional visits to the racecourse and typically means that they have some kind of physical problem that requires careful management and may sometimes interrupt their training regime. (This sort of issue can, of course, afflict human athletes and sports people, too.) Expertly handled, such horses can have successful careers, and may run pretty much to their best when they are 'right'.

Head-carriage   The manner in which a horse carries his head and neck when racing (and in other equestrian sports) is of some significance. Observers of galloping horses like to see the head and neck carried stretched a little forward, with something of a convex arch and the horse's face angled downward, somewhere towards the perpendicular. These features suggest that the horse is travelling well, is balanced, and is not fighting the jockey. Forms of head-carriage other than this may provide different indications:

- *The head and neck stretched forward*, in a more-or-less straight line, suggest that the horse is travelling at the maximum speed he can raise at that time. This is not necessarily bad, if it happens in the closing stages of the race and the horse is in contention – indeed, it may show that he is trying really hard – however, it's not an encouraging sight if it indicates that he is flat-out at an earlier stage of the race.

- *Some horses gallop with their head and neck very low* – in some cases, the nose is not far off the ground. This is sometimes viewed as demonstrating willingness but – while it is unlikely to demonstrate the opposite – there can be various causes. It may be connected to how the horse relates to the bit in his mouth (in which case a change of bit may be in order); it may be related to the **conformation** of his shoulders and neck, and the angle at which his skull attaches to his neck ('head set on low', in which case nothing can be done); and it may be related to his overall balance. Regarding the last, a horse who carries more weight than ideal on his front end (is 'on the forehand') will move less efficiently than a better balanced horse. This will not necessarily prevent him from winning races, but it is not a plus. A very low head-carriage can have an influence on the jockey (although it's preferable to a horse who is fighting and throwing his head around). If it is significantly related to balance, it can make the horse 'heavy' in the hand and, for a steeplechase jockey, galloping towards a fence with the horse's head almost on the ground can be quite 'interesting'. (That said, sometimes a horse who runs like this will jump quite adequately, but it is perhaps helpful if the jockey is familiar with the horse's style and takes account of it in his own riding at the fences – *see also* **sees a stride**.)

This horse is going to the start with his head very high – his jockey will be hoping to get him to lower it as soon as possible.

- *A horse who throws his head about* is resisting his jockey's attempts to get him settled and may also be compromising the jockey's efforts to adopt the desired tactics. The horse will, undoubtedly, be wasting nervous energy and, if the head-throwing is violent he will actually be unbalancing himself. Despite doing this, a horse will sometimes win the race if the action is fairly short-lived and he is superior to the opposition, but his career is unlikely to progress significantly unless he can learn to **settle**.
- *A horse who combines throwing his head about with carrying it high* is almost certainly trying to evade the rider's restraint but, although he may well be trying to go faster, he is actually putting himself in a bad posture from which to do this really effectively. Because the neck is a continuation of the spine, the concave shape caused in the neck by raising the head will tend to be replicated in the spine. This positioning (called a 'hollow outline' in other branches of equitation) blocks, to some extent, the forward thrust of the horse's hindquarters from propelling him forward with maximum power. Thus, while a horse in this position may be moving very 'busily' he will not be moving to best effect. For a jump jockey in particular, a horse moving in this way offers various challenges. In the first place, the horse may not be concentrating on the job in hand (which includes sizing up the obstacles) and his high/unsteady head-carriage will not assist his view of them. Secondly, the head-carriage may also interfere with the jockey's view. Thirdly, when a horse is moving in this mechanically inefficient way, it is very hard for a rider to adjust his stride by truly shortening or lengthening it. He may be able to slow the horse down, or speed him up, but that is not the same thing. Galloping at a steeplechase fence on a horse moving in this manner is not many jockeys' idea of fun.
- *A high head-carriage* is, for many people, a major negative in the closing stages of a race, because they interpret it simply as a sign of unwillingness on a horse's part. To be clear, sticking his head in the air is a common characteristic of a non-compliant horse, in racing and elsewhere, and it can never be seen as a positive. However, because there may be other factors involved, it cannot simply be assumed that a horse who does this is necessarily what used to be called a 'rogue'. Other possible factors could include such things as a sinus infection, a bad tooth, or significant discomfort with the bit. Another is that the horse may have an incipient breathing problem and be trying instinctively to find a way of taking in more air. (Thus the possibility exists that, far from showing unwillingness, a horse who does this when asked for maximum effort is actually trying to comply.) In recent years, trainers have become far more aware of breathing problems in racing, and keen to investigate and treat them. Some conditions respond quite positively to relatively minor surgery and a number of horses who had previously lost their form have recaptured it following treatment. One other reason for a higher-than-normal head-carriage may be the opposite of one mentioned in connection with horses who gallop with a low head-carriage for skeletal reasons – in this case, the head is set on high. Again, nothing can be done about this and, as long as it is not associated with other issues, horses built in this manner should be capable of performing to their optimum.

Hit a flat spot   Said of a horse who, having been travelling comfortably, suddenly needs to be ridden along. This would apply to most horses in the closing stages of a race, but the intended reference is to an earlier stage. Some very good horses have been known to do this regularly before coming back **on the bridle**. It may be, in some cases, that they are just laid-back individuals, but it is possible that there is sometimes an underlying physical reason for this behaviour.

Hold-up horse   Not the mount of a highwayman, but a horse whose running style is such that he is best restrained in the early part of the race, to conserve his energy and/or capitalize on his ability to accelerate in the closing stages. (*See also* **delivered late** and **waiting race**.)

Idling   A trait of some horses who, once they hit the front, reduce their response to the jockey and, typically, flick their ears back and forth and perhaps begin to look around. Distinct from simply getting tired, these actions suggest that a horse feels that, having taken the lead, he has done enough and/or that he is 'looking for company'. In the latter case, once such a horse is challenged by a rival, he may start to race again in earnest. Jockeys on horses known to do this will try to avoid taking the lead too soon, and **connections** of those in whom the trait is ingrained may fit headgear to try to focus concentration.

In a pocket   Said of a horse with rivals in front of him and to the side. In such a situation, his jockey will have to find a way to extricate himself without transcending the rules of racing (i.e. by barging his way out). This typically means waiting for a gap to appear because one of the surrounding opponents has either weakened and dropped back, or accelerated ahead.

In the country   An old term referring to parts of a racecourse remote from the grandstand.

In the frame   This old phrase refers to the practice of putting the numbers of placed horses in a physical frame near the winning post and raising it to show the result,

Jump off   In a racing context, this simply means start the race promptly, as in 'he jumped off **on terms** with the others'.

Keen   Describes a horse who is racing a little more enthusiastically than might be considered ideal, but is not really fighting his jockey, or on the verge of **running away**. Sometimes, a jockey may be satisfied by having his horse in this state, reasoning that a greater attempt to restrain the horse could result in counterproductive resistance.

Length in principle, a length is the approximate length of a horse, which we could say is round about 8½ft. Of course, horses are actually different sizes and their *apparent* length will also depend on the extent to which they are extended or collected during their stride pattern. If you watch one horse following another during a race and the commentator says the leading horse is 'about three lengths clear' you will usually be able to see for yourself that, give or take a small margin, that looks pretty much right. However, the official 'lengths' between horses recorded at the finish of a race are not strictly horse lengths, but are based on some pretty complex calculations by which the *time* between the horses passing the post is converted to '*lengths*'. The bases for these calculations vary between flat turf, flat all-weather and jumping surfaces, and

The changing outline of a galloping horse – in the collected/suspension phase of his stride, and extending as he lands on his forelegs.

Shorter Winning Margins

On the subject of distances, the shorter winning margins in common use are three-quarters of a length, half a length, a neck, a head, a short head and a nose. These should be short enough to be recorded pretty accurately. The first two should be self-evident; a neck means that one horse won by about the distance of his extended head and neck; a head means about the length of that alone; a short head means a bit less than that and a nose means about the length from the horse's nostril to his lips.

are adjusted for variations in going, but not for race distance. It would, of course, be incredibly difficult to record accurately the definitive distance between all the finishers in a race of any complexity. However, reported distances in between horses, in 'lengths', especially longer margins in longer races, should be recognized as approximate.

Lost his action   Said of a horse whose stride pattern has become significantly compromised; usually a sign of lameness or another physical problem, although it can happen momentarily if a horse is impeded, or hits a patch of false ground.

Lost his form   In racing, this term is not used in the human athletic sense of a runner losing their stride pattern, but in the sense that recent results have been below standard. There are numerous reasons why this might happen to a horse, and a good trainer will make strenuous efforts to find the root cause and effect a remedy. (Sometimes, this can happen to a number of horses in a trainer's yard in a short space of time, for reasons such as a low-grade virus circulating the yard, a batch of feed with a nutritional deficiency, etc.).

Not letting himself down *see* **feeling the ground.**

Odds on   A price shorter than **even money**. This is usually written with the figures reversed: two to one on is thus 1–2. In this case, the win is half the original stake, thus £5 at 1–2 will see you get back £7.50 (£5 stake plus £2.50 win).

Official handicappers   The team employed by the BHA, whose job it is to convert their assessment of horses' racing performances into numerical form (*see* **ratings**).

Off the bridle   The horse is not moving powerfully into the jockey's hands – the opposite of **on the bridle.**

On a long rein   If a horse is rather tense before the start of a race, the jockey may ride him around at walk with long reins (sometimes with his own legs hanging down out of the stirrups). This mimics what happens after horses have been exercised at home and the horse may perceive it as a signal to relax. Sometimes, also, either when cantering to the start or in the actual race, a jockey may ride with longer reins than are usually associated with race-riding. This takes a cool nerve, but again can help some horses to relax mentally. Such horses tend to associate a tighter, shorter hold on the reins with being a signal to quicken – in fact, this shorter hold on the reins ('picking the horse up') is common practice in race-riding when the jockey is about to ask for maximum effort, but some horses are very sensitive to the reins being shortened at moments when maximum effort is not required.

One-paced   Said of a horse who lacks the ability to accelerate to any significant degree.

On terms   Means that a horse is racing pretty much with others as the race commences and during in the race.

On the bridle   The horse is travelling comfortably, without being urged along by the jockey.

Outsider   A horse so-called because he is deemed to have only an 'outside' chance of winning, and will therefore be at long odds. Both 'outsider' and 'long odds' are relative terms: in a small field, a horse whose odds are 8–1 could be an outsider (perhaps the outsider of the whole field) but in a competitive race with a big field, the same odds could represent a well-fancied runner. In a race such as the Grand National, 20–1 would not represent 'outsider' odds – the term would be more appropriately applied to horses whose odds were perhaps 33–1 upwards. An old, rather disrespectful term for an outsider is 'the rag'.
  Outsiders do sometimes win, or feature prominently in races, *despite being* rather than *because they are* outsiders.

Pacemaker   A horse entered in a race with the primary intention of setting the pace (ensuring a true gallop) for another runner. Pacemakers are contentious and there are rules about how they participate – for example, they are not allowed to interfere with other runners and they should not ease the passage of the horse for whom they are setting the pace. Furthermore, it is a rule of racing that every horse should run on his own merits, and be ridden to obtain the best possible placing, so there are those who claim that, in fact, this is not always the case with pacemakers. If a pacemaker is to fulfil his role it is important (particularly in shorter flat races), that he gets away from the start promptly, and it is also important that his jockey does not set such a strong pace that the other runners ignore him, knowing that his horse will 'run out of petrol' well before the closing stages. (There have been a few occasions when a pacemaker has made all the running and held on to win the race, which is both ironic and amusing.)

Photo finish   The use of photography rather than just the judge's eyes to determine the result of a close finish to a race first appeared in the UK in 1947, being initially used only on the flat. Technology has advanced considerably since those early days and it is now possible for a winner to be determined by a very narrow margin (sometimes described as 'a couple of pixels') on an enlarged digital image. A judge will nowadays call for a photo whenever the perceived winning margin is considered to be a head or less. The equipment now used to provide such images is also used to compute the finishing margins between horses in a race. (*See also* **length**.)

Placed   What this can mean in a betting context (i.e. whether or not an each way bet on the horse would have been successful) is explained in the panel 'Placed' and Place Odds in Chapter 6.

Plants   Said of a horse who refuses point-blank to go forwards. This sometimes happens on leaving the paddock to go down to the start, in which case the horse may be persuaded to move either by having another runner to follow, or being led briefly by his handler. (In some cases, the jockey may jump off and lead the horse down in to the start in hand.) It can also happen at the start, in which case, even if the horse is finally persuaded to **jump off**, he will probably have forfeited too much ground to get involved in the race.

Pulling   This has some similarities with the horse who is fighting for his head by throwing it about, but exists on a more subtle level. A horse who is pulling is working very strongly into the bit (and may thus test his jockey's arms), but this tends to suggest an eagerness to get on with things rather than an uncooperative 'strop' on his part. However, a horse who pulls too hard for too long will compromise his chances by using up too much energy.

Ratings   An official rating is the number allotted to every horse to represent the **official handicapper's** assessment of the horse's current ability. These ratings, which may be raised or lowered depending on the handicapper's reaction to a horse's recent form (or lack of it, if the horse has been out of action for some time), provide the basis for determining which races a horse is eligible to run in, and the weight he will be allotted in a handicap. (In the latter case, the actual weight he will be given will depend on the class of the handicap and a comparison to the ratings of other horses that have been entered – the fact that a horse has a rating of X doesn't mean of itself that he will necessarily carry Y stone in any race.)

There are separate ratings for flat racing (sometimes also variations for individual horses between turf and all-weather) and NH racing. In all cases, the higher the number, the better the horse is rated but, although the number range for the different **codes** overlaps, the same rating figure will (a bit like Fahrenheit and Centigrade temperatures) signify something different between them. To give a *very broad* illustration of the differences between flat and NH ratings, Frankel, the highest-rated flat horse in recent years, had a rating of around 140, whereas the best jumpers of their generation are often rated above 170. Thus, a horse rated 125+ on the flat will be nearly a top-level performer, whereas the same rating figure over jumps would suggest a pretty ordinary performer. It is therefore evident that (despite the fact that some dual-purpose horses perform relatively better either on the flat or over hurdles) it is unlikely that a horse would have the same (or even that similar) a rating under both codes.

It's worth noting that some racing journals have their own systems of ratings, which are often given alongside the official ones. The latter can usually be identified by the code OR (official rating).

Return   The money to come back from a bet. This is not necessarily the same as 'winnings', which suggests that you get back more than you put on. Returns could mean, for example, that you have £16 to come back from an each way bet that cost you £20.

Returned at …   A phrase that refers to a horse's starting price, e.g.: 'He was returned at 14–1.'

Round course   This doesn't mean that the course is actually circular (although Chester comes fairly close); it is used to distinguish that part of the track that forms a circuit, as opposed to the straight section leading up to the winning line. Under this description, most courses in the UK have a 'round' component, although there are exceptions such as Brighton and Epsom, which are more or less U-shaped, and Newmarket, which has two flat courses, both with just a single bend. Both Goodwood and Salisbury have looped layouts, which are not strictly 'round' courses, and the flat course at Windsor and the steeplechase course at Fontwell have circuits in the form of a figure of eight.

Run green   Green is used here in the context of inexperience. An inexperienced racehorse may reduce his chances of performing to best effect by such actions as **dwelling** at the start, not jumping fluently in a NH race, looking around rather than giving his full concentration to racing, running off a straight line, not wishing to go past other horses, or slowing down if he hits the front. Even having exhibited some of these traits, a horse who runs green will sometimes win the race.

Run(ing) in snatches   A term used to describe a horse whose running style throughout a race varies between being on and off the bridle – at some stages he is travelling comfortably; at others he needs urging along. The reasons behind this may be either physical or psychological, or perhaps a mixture. (*See also* **hit a flat spot.**)

Running away   This term has similarities to **bolted up**. Although it can be used to describe a horse who has taken charge of his rider, it is more often used figuratively to describe one who seems to be travelling very much better than his rivals during a race.

Seeing too much daylight   Some horses perform best if they can be settled in behind rivals in the early stages of a race, so that they relax better and conserve their energy for the later stages. If the jockey of such a horse is unable to do this (perhaps as a result of an unfavourable draw, or because the tactics/positioning of other riders make it difficult), the horse will 'see too much daylight', race too keenly, and fade in the closing stages.

Sees a stride   In any form of competition that involves jumping (whether human or equine), the ability to 'see a stride' is a great asset, since it maximizes the chances of jumping the obstacles safely and fluently. With riding, the jumping aspect ideally includes a degree of rapport between rider and horse and, the more there is, the better the prospects for the partnership. Horses, through a combination of temperament and physique, will tend to have their optimum way of jumping. Some are naturally bold and flamboyant; some are naturally more careful; some have a high degree of jumping power ('scope') and/or a natural ability to adjust their jump according to circumstances; others have less of these qualities and need to exercise prudence – even a level of caution – in their jumping. A horse with 'nous' will tend to have more of an aptitude for adjusting his stride on the approach to a fence so that he meets it on a reasonable stride than one who doesn't, and a rider with a good 'eye' and an instinctive rapport with horses will be most effective in tuning in to a horse's preferred way of jumping and riding him accordingly.

Settled   Said of a horse who is moving comfortably without either fighting his jockey or needing to be pushed along.

Shade of the odds   A term sometimes used to refer to very minor differences in odds offered by bookmakers. The principle of fractional odds is explained in the panel Understanding Odds in Chapter 6, and the same principle can sometimes be used to produce odds that seem rather – well, 'odd'. One example, formerly seen on occasion but now very rare, was 85–40, which 'boils down' to $2^{1}/_{8}$–1, and is thus slightly longer than 2–1 and slightly shorter than 9–4 (which boils down to 2¼–1). With a little practice, it is easy to 'read' at least the general message of such odds – for example 11–10 is clearly slightly longer than **even money**, and 5–6 is slightly **odds on**.

Spread a plate   The light shoes worn by racehorses are known as racing plates. These are relatively flimsy compared to conventional shoes, and can sometimes become loose ('spread') while a horse is cantering to the start. All courses have a farrier on hand to deal with this eventuality, so there is an option to have the faulty shoe replaced before the race. Connections can opt in advance to say whether, if a horse spreads a plate (or actually loses a shoe), he should be reshod or withdrawn from the race. This covers horses who perhaps have 'tricky' feet and require some special attention when they are shod.

Stake   The amount of money you place on a bet. When cash betting with a course or High Street bookie, you hand this over as you place your bet. If the bet loses, the bookie keeps it; if the bet wins, you get the stake returned along with your actual winnings. (The term 'Stakes' as part of a race name relates to entry costs and has nothing to do with betting on the race.)

Takes a pull   Said of a jockey who restrains his horse briefly, because he doesn't want to get involved in a battle for the lead sooner than suits the horse's style of running.

Taking a hold   The horse is **keen** to the extent of resisting the jockey's attempts to restrain him – i.e. he is trying to go faster than desired.

The field   The runners in a race. However, in a betting context, this means something different – for example '4–1 the field' *doesn't* mean that all the horses in the race are 4–1; it is a bookies' way of saying that 4–1 is the shortest price in the race, i.e. the price of the favourite/joint favourites.

The market   The weight of money bet on a race, which will impact upon the odds. For example, a phrase such as 'the market got it wrong' signifies that the favourite (or sometimes several fancied horses) performed less well than punters expected.

The run-in   In a race over jumps, the part of the course from the final obstacle to the finishing line.

Trapped wide   A commentator's description of a horse who, as the runners negotiate a bend, is to the outside of most of the field. Some commentators seem almost to obsess about this, but it's rather a question of degree and circumstance. Simple geometry tells us that, if a number of horses are going round a bend, those on the inside are travelling a shorter distance than those out wide and, if the bend is quite tight, or prolonged, the difference in distance can be quite significant. However, in some circumstances, being just a couple of horses wide may have its own advantages, for example:

- On soft/heavy going, the ground just wide of the inside rail may offer a better surface than the ground close to it.
- A horse being taken a little wide into the finishing straight is more likely to have a clear run home than a rival who is trapped behind others on the rail.
- Some horses dislike being crowded by their rivals, and travel better when they have some room around them, so the jockey on such a horse may opt to go a little wide for this reason. This does rely on the jockey knowing the horse's preference, because some horses who **see too much daylight** out wide may get too **keen** and over-race. Also, perhaps oddly, some horses actually enjoy being caught up in a crowd and may not perform to their optimum if asked to race in isolation.
(*See also* **drawn/posted wide.**)

Trip   The distance of a race.

Unplaced   This term is logically the opposite of **placed** but, as explained in the panel 'Placed' and Place Odds' in Chapter 6, that is subject to interpretation in different circumstances, and thus unplaced is too. For example, a horse who finishes third in a seven-runner race would probably be referred to 'placed' by people using the term casually (i.e. to mean 'first, second or third'), even though each way bets on him would be lost. In this respect, ITV racing coverage has adopted the system of giving results by stipulating the horses placed for betting purposes, and identifying any other 'placed' horses 'for information'. For example, in reporting the result of the seven-runner race just mentioned, they would give the first and second, with their starting prices, and add the name of the third horse 'for information only'.

Waiting race   A jockey is said to be 'riding a waiting race' when he is intentionally keeping his horse to a greater or lesser extent behind other runners. There are several underlying reasons why a jockey may do this, but they relate, in essence, to trying to conserve energy and/or hoping to use a horse's ability to accelerate as a trump card in the closing stages. (*See also* **hold-up horse.**)

Weighing room   The room in which jockeys prepare for a race and are weighed before and after the race to check that they will be riding/have ridden at the correct weight.

Weight allowance   Can refer either to weight concessions for certain types of horses (*see* Categories of Races in Chapter 2) or for apprentice/conditional/amateur jockeys (*see* Jockeys in Chapter 3).

Index